The Moors of the Southwest 2 Exploring the Ancient Tracks of Dartmoor, Bodmin and Penwith

'

As a journalist specializing in education, Shirley Toulson worked on the staff of the NUT journal *The Teacher*, and edited the monthly magazine *Child Education* from 1970 to 1974. Since then she has concentrated on writing books concerned with the social history and folklore of the countryside. She has lived in Somerset since 1980, but spends the summer months visiting the places connected with the series of books she is currently preparing on the migrations and pilgrimages of the early Christian Celts. She has written and published occasional poems since the 1950s, and now reviews poetry regularly for the British Council and the *South West Arts Review*.

Roughton

The Moors of the Southwest
2 Exploring the Ancient Tracks of Dartmoor, Bodmin and Penwith

Shirley Toulson

Illustrated by Oliver Caldecott
Maps drawn by Sue Lawes

Hutchinson
London Melbourne Sydney Auckland Johannesburg

By the same author

Discovering Farms and Farm Museums

The Drovers' Roads of Wales

East Anglia: Walking the Ley Lines and
Ancient Tracks

Derbyshire: Exploring the Ancient Tracks
and Mysteries of Mercia

The Winter Solstice

The Moors of the Southwest: I Exploring the
Ancient Tracks of Sedgemoor and Exmoor

Hutchinson & Co. (Publishers) Ltd

An imprint of the Hutchinson Publishing Group

17–21 Conway Street, London W1P 6JD

Hutchinson Publishing Group (Australia) Pty Ltd
PO Box 496, 16–22 Church Street, Hawthorne,
Melbourne, Victoria 3122

Hutchinson Group (NZ) Ltd
32–34 View Road, PO Box 40–086, Glenfield,
Auckland 10

Hutchinson Group (SA) Pty Ltd
PO Box 337, Bergvlei 2012, South Africa

First published as a Hutchinson Paperback 1984
Text © Shirley Toulson 1984
Illustrations © Oliver Caldecott 1984
Maps © Sue Lawes 1984

Set in VIP Century Schoolbook by
D. P. Media Limited, Hitchin, Hertfordshire

Printed and bound in Great Britain
by Anchor Brendon Ltd, of Tiptree, Essex

British Library Cataloguing in Publication Data

Toulson, Shirley
  Moors of the Southwest.
  2: Exploring the ancient tracks of
  Dartmoor, Bodmin and Penwith.
  1. Walking–West Country (England)
  2. West Country (England)–Description and
travel–Guidebooks
  I. Title
  796.5'1'09423   DA670.W9
ISBN 0 09 151881 4

Contents

The Cheesewring

Acknowledgements

I should like to express my thanks to the Field Studies Council for allowing me to use their centre at Slapton Ley for my initial work on Dartmoor, and for making their library there available to me; to the Dartmoor National Park's walk leaders, some of whose expeditions I joined, and who were invariably helpful and patient with my inquiries; and to Mr H. L. Douch of the County Museum at Truro for the information he gave me.

I am grateful too to the many old friends and walking companions who have helped me with my investigations and explorations; and I should especially like to mention my cousin, Martha Stevenson of Manaton, whose long acquaintance with Dartmoor was of invaluable help to me.

Note

For the reader's convenience I have substituted the OS sheet numbers for the more usual National Grid letters with each map reference.

The maps in this book are based on personal observation. They will help you to follow the walks in the book and to pick out the salient features on them but they are not accurate as to scale or topography, nor do they include contours. All walkers are therefore urged to equip themselves in addition with Ordnance Survey maps, either 1:25,000 or 1:50,000 scale.

KEY TO MAPS

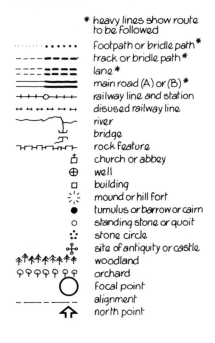

* heavy lines show route to be followed
Footpath or bridle path *
track or bridle path *
lane *
main road (A) or (B) *
railway line and station
disused railway line
river
bridge
rock feature
church or abbey
well
building
mound or hill fort
tumulus or barrow or cairn
standing stone or quoit
stone circle
site of antiquity or castle
woodland
orchard
focal point
alignment
north point

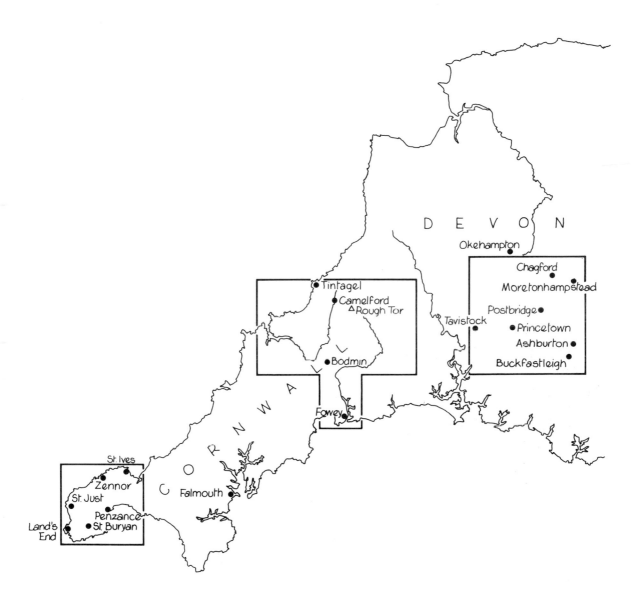

D E V O N

Okehampton

Chagford
Moretonhampstead
Postbridge
Tavistock
Princetown
Ashburton
Buckfastleigh

Tintagel
Camelford
△ Rough Tor

Bodmin

Fowey

C O R N W A L L

St. Ives
Zennor
St. Just
Penzance
St Buryan
Land's
End

Falmouth

GENERAL MAP

Hut circle
Dartmoor

10

Introduction: Granite

I remember being at a ball many years ago at that epoch in the development of woman when her 'body' was hooked along her dorsal ridge. Now I learn from competent authorities that it is held together in other fashion.

There was at the ball a very lusty stout lady in slate-grey satin.

By nature and age, assisted by victuals, she was unadapted to take violent exercise. Nevertheless dance she would. Dance she did until there ensued an explosion. Hooks, eyes, buttons, yielded and there ensued an eruption of subjacent materials. In places the fastenings held so that the tumescent under-garments foamed out at intervals in large bulging masses.

This is precisely what took place with Mother Earth in one of her gambols. Her slate panoply gave way, parted from N.E. to S.W., and out burst the granite, which had been kept under and was not intended for show.

Her hooks and eyes gave way first of all in South Devon, and out swelled the great mass of Dartmoor. They held for a little space, and then out broke another mass that constitutes the Bodmin moors. It heaved to the surface again north of St Austell, then was held back as far as Redruth and Camborne. A few more hooks remained firm, and then the garment gave way for the Land's End district, and finally, out of the sea it shows again in Scilly.

Sabine Baring-Gould,
A Book of the West: Cornwall, 1899

Baring-Gould's analogy comes a little curiously from the pen of a Victorian cleric, yet it has given me a far better idea of the eruption of the granite masses of the Southwest than any more precise geological description I have come across. The scientific facts, however, are more romantic than he allows, for these bosses of igneous rock have unfathomed bases, which extend in some places well beneath the earth's crust, and whose tops burst through the rough grass and heather of the moorland hills. And these 'under-garments' are embroidered with quart, mica and white or pinkish felspar, and adorned with rich mineral deposits.

Of the six granite eruptions listed by Baring-Gould, Dartmoor is by far the largest, covering an area of 248 square miles. The other two which I have included in this book are Bodmin (80 square miles) and the Penwith area around Land's End (some 75 square miles).

Although the last area is the smallest of the three, it is the richest in the minerals which are to be found in granites, produced by the gases emanating from the hot lava as it pushed its way through the earth's crust. Millions of years later, those deposits were to affect the whole course of the history of this southwest extremity of Britain. For it was Cornish tin, which supplanted the smaller deposits of Spain, that made the British peninsula the trading centre of the ancient world, which depended on that metal to advance its technology as we depend on oil.

The deposits of tin on Dartmoor were not discovered until the twelfth century. Then throughout the Middle Ages the wealth from the tin of the Southwest was once again such an important part of the economy of the whole country that the tin miners became a law unto themselves, being granted special rights and privileges by royal decree. They had their own Stannary Parliament (a name derived from the Latin word for tin), which many Cornishmen today think should be actively revived. Until 1305 the tinners' delegates met on Hingston Down, just to the west of the

Introduction: Granite

Tamar; but in that year the men of Devon formed their own parliament, which met on or near Crockern Tor in the centre of Dartmoor. There they met for about four hundred years, until the Stannary Parliament of Dartmoor was moved to Tavistock. The decrees issued by these parliaments had all the sanction of law. Under a charter granted to the miners in the reign of Edward I, the delegates to the Stannary Parliaments had power over all matters relating to the mines, and had the right to imprison anybody who broke their laws. In Cornwall the Stannary prison was at Lostwithiel; on Dartmoor it was at Lydford.

Until shafts were sunk for the first time in the early sixteenth century, tin was produced by streaming, the process of separating the pebbles containing the tin from the clods of loose earth by washing them in running water. After that the metal was extracted from the stone by being subjected to intense heat. This smelting, which was originally done by piling the stones in holes in the ground and lighting fires on top of them, was later carried out in blowing houses in which the furnace was kept blazing by bellows operated by a small water wheel. Ruins of these blowing houses are to be found all over Dartmoor; many of them stand beside the waters of leats or small channels that are still running and which originally provided the power to work the furnace.

Apart from tin, the two most common byproducts of granite are copper and china clay. The former, which appears at the junction of granite and slate, was worked in the far west of Cornwall from the fifteenth century, while the much smaller deposit on Dartmoor was not mined until the nineteenth. China clay, which is made up of decomposed felspar mixed with mica and quartz, has been quarried most extensively in the area around St Austell, where the landscape is now composed of a range of shimmering white mountains. There are lesser, but rapidly expanding, workings on Bodmin and Dartmoor.

For the people who have lived on all these moors since the time of the Bronze Age, and probably long before that, the granite itself has been the chief natural resource. The generations have pirated each other's work, farmers using any convenient blocks from ancient ritual sites when they needed a gate post; but there are still masses of loose granite chunks, broken pieces of tor, lying about on the hillside for anyone who has the tenement rights in the area and the skill and strength to remove them. Many of these rocks are scored by the chisels of stone masons who exercised that privilege and obtained their raw material from the moors.

The walks across the five granite moors follow the trade routes of the tinners and trace the patterns on the landscape drawn out by the men who sited the religious monuments of the Bronze Age, and by Richard Long, a contemporary artist, who has used the ancient designs for his own purposes. Pattern and trade route are both combined in the tracks that run from the east to Land's End itself. This 'long-distance path' has become known as the 'dragon' line, partly because it was thought to follow a ley line which ran diagonally across England from the Wash through Stonehenge towards the Scilly Isles; and partly because it passes through so many churches dedicated to St Michael, Archangel and slayer of dragons. The line enters the granite moors at East Week, a village on the northeast edge of Dartmoor, and goes through the southern part of Bodmin Moor and along the central ridge of Penwith. East Week is one of the few places on Dartmoor where Neolithic material has been discovered, and it is tempting and fairly reasonable to believe that it stood on a Stone Age trading route that went diagonally across England.

As Christianity became established, crosses replaced the standing stones and barrows as waymarks and boundary posts. Often these two purposes were combined, and sometimes an original pagan stone was christened by the rough inscription of a cross. The patterns of these crosses vary. In Penwith, the rounded 'four-holed' cross, in which the arms are encircled by stone, is common; on Dartmoor, the arms of the crosses usually stand clear without any surrounding stone.

These crosses have never completely exorcised the pagan spirit of the moors. It lives on in myths and legends combining the fables of the Christian Arthur and those of the miracles wrought by the

Tremowran Hill Fort.

Celtic saints with tales of giants and pixies. The giants haunt Cornwall, and as Gerald Priestland suggests (*West of Hayle River*, Wildwood House, 1980), they probably originated in stories, passed down by the little men of the Bronze Age, about the tall Celts, with their mysterious iron implements, who gradually took over the moors. The pixies who inhabit Dartmoor come from the opposite source. They probably owe their existence to the Bronze Age people themselves, who took refuge from the Celtic and Saxon farmers by hiding in their old settlements on the most remote parts of the moor, only daring to emerge at night.

Yet these same Celts, the tribe of the Dumnovi, had a reputation for kindly hospitality. In 300 BC the Greek traveller and geographer Pytheas described them as 'friendly to strangers' and their descendants still have that characteristic, although it does not imply that they absorb strangers easily into their own communities. If you come from anywhere east of Somerset, you walk here as a 'grockle' or an 'emmett', and as such your activities can become as much part of the folklore as the habits of giants and pixies.

Yet you will be in good company. For thousands of years people from the east have walked across these moors to the most southwesterly point of Britain. The walks in this book are the logical continuations of the ones we embarked on in Somerset, where we left the dragon line at Creech St Michael on the outskirts of Taunton. On those walks we looked southwest from the heights of Exmoor to the granite cliffs of Dartmoor and the continuation of that ancient route. Now we follow it again as it crosses Dartmoor above Okehampton and leaves it at the hilltop church of St Michael de Rupe (of the rock) at Brent Tor. From there we follow its course past Bronze Age circles and Iron Age villages on the moors of Bodmin and Penwith, until it eventually reaches the sea and whatever drowned land lies beneath the waves that separate the Cornish mainland from the Scilly Isles.

Part One Dartmoor

Focal Points

Beardown Man 191: 590795
Bennett's Cross 191: 684816
Brent Tor 191: 471805
Buckfast Abbey 202: 742674
Cawsand Beacon 191: 635915
Childe's Tomb 202: 626704
Corringdon Ball 202: 669614
Devil's Rock, Dewerstone 201: 539640
East Week 191: 665920
Gibbet Hill 191: 503813
Grey Wethers 191: 638832
Grimspound 191: 701809
Haytor Rocks 191: 757770
Hembury Castle 202: 726684
Hound Tor 191: 743790
Hunter's Tor 191: 762824
Huntingdon Cross 202: 665661
Jay's Grave 191: 733799
Kestor 191: 665864
Lydford Church 191: 509848
Modbury 202: 655515
Moreleigh 202: 762526
Nun's Cross Farm 202: 605698
Petre's Cross 202: 655655
Scorhill Circle 191: 655875
Shaugh Prior 201: 543632
Sheepstor 202: 561676
Spinsters' Rock 191: 700908
Warren House Inn 191: 674809
Watern Oke 191: 566834
Whitchurch Priory 201: 488730
White Barrow 191: 565794
White Moor Stone Circle 191: 633897
Widecombe Church 191: 719768
Wistman's Wood 191: 613774
Yes Tor 191: 580903

Bennett's Cross

Part One Dartmoor

I solemnly swear to you, Sir, nothing will ever induce me to set foot on Dartmoor again. If I chance to see it from the Hoe, Sir, I'll avert my eyes. How can people think to come here for pleasure – for pleasure, Sir! But there Chinamen eat birds' nests. There are depraved appetites among human beings, and only unwholesome minded individuals can love Dartmoor.

A tailor of Plymouth to Sabine Baring-Gould on being found lost on the slopes of Mis Tor
A Book of Dartmoor, 1900

Exmoor I know and love. To Dartmoor I am a stranger and respectful. And even when driving to Plymouth from North Devon one is careful only to skirt the Moor, travelling by Sourton and Blackdown, Horrabridge and Yelverton.

Jeremy Thorpe, Introduction to Clive Gunnell's *My Dartmoor*, 1980

Those two gentlemen are not alone in having found Dartmoor to be a fearful stretch of wilderness. The Romans hated the place and were not even tempted to try to civilize it despite the suspicion, which they must have had from their knowledge of Cornish tin, that rich mineral deposits lay in the granite. I too must confess that when I only drove across the moor, the journey was uneasy. It was as though some force in that barren upland resented my presence. When I started walking across it my mood changed, for I discovered a landscape of enchanting beauty. Even in clear weather the place demands an aware respect, but in my experience that is not due to any supernatural malignant force, but simply because the powers of nature are alien and impersonal, and in such a wilderness they can harm as well as please.

The true mystery of the moor comes from the 'old men', the people who lived here during the Bronze Age, when the weather was warm enough for their farms to support many families. In clearing the original woodland for intense cultivation they started the process of erosion, which has resulted in the great peat blanket – which now covers the northern heights of the moor – and the quaking bogs – which are both a discomfort and a danger to the walker.

The extent of their farming enterprises can be judged by the numerous cattle kraals and the settlement enclosures where the remains of the huts still stand, as well as by the cists and cairns in which the important dead were buried, and the numerous stone circles and puzzling stone rows which mark the sacred sites. And all of these represent only a fraction of the Bronze Age building on the moor, for many of the sacred pillars have been used for gate posts, and the granite blocks, once so carefully arranged, have been taken for farm buildings. Douglas St Leger Gordon, who lived at Sticklepath on the northern edge of the moor, reported the loss of two circles in that area, one of which was being dismantled by a local stone mason within living memory.

That sort of pragmatic vandalism probably started with the Saxons. The barrows, however, were subjected to another sort of greed when the people in the early Middle Ages, avid for the treasure that was said to lie within them, started tomb robbing. Stories of buried crocks of gold

Stone circle, Dartmoor

abounded, but it is unlikely that much of that metal was ever to be found among the Bronze Age grave goods on Dartmoor. Yet the rumour that great wealth lay in the barrows persisted, and it was strong enough to persuade Edward II to make a grant out of his exchequer for the purpose of opening up the grave mounds in Devonshire.

It was the fashionable interest in antiquarian studies in the eighteenth and nineteenth centuries that saved most of the Bronze Age relics from destruction. The diggers were often as hurried and clumsy as the early tomb robbers, and many of their historical theories were wild; but we owe a lot to the energy and determination of such gentlemen as the Reverend Sabine Baring-Gould. Most of his work was undertaken during the late nineteenth century, and his researches made him aware of the extent of the early population of the

moor and the importance of preserving the monuments of a lost civilization for posterity. He wrote sharply about a fellow divine, the Reverend W. Davy, an eighteenth-century vicar of Drewsteignton, who put all his energies into compiling theological treatises. 'At Drewsteignton there was a most remarkable collection of stone circles and avenues and menhirs, and all have gone now, not one's left, only the dolmen of Shilstone remains,' he complained, angrily noting that 'One accurate plan drawn by Davy, and plan he could, would have been worth all his twenty-six volumes of *Systems of Divinity.*'

The dolmen at Shilstone that Baring-Gould referred to is known as Spinster's Rock and is much older than any Bronze Age remains in the area. It is one of the few Neolithic remains on the moor, for although there are certainly signs that

Stone Age men lived and hunted here, they did so in far fewer numbers than the farmers with their bronze and copper implements who succeeded them.

Those settlements do not seem to have been usurped by the Iron Age Celts, who built most of their farms on the edges of the moor. The Saxon farmers of Dartmoor followed that example, but they and their descendants grazed their animals on the uplands in summer, and kept them indoors in part of their own houses during the worst of the winter. Traces of those longhouses, shared by beasts and men, can still be seen in some of the old farm buildings on the moor. Originally the building was arranged so that the family lived on one side of a central culvert, and the animals on the other.

It was in the early Middle Ages that the land of the moor was apportioned into tenements and the grazing rights codified, with the result that now there is no truly common land on Dartmoor. The people who graze their animals there do so by a modification of the ancient right of *venville*, which gave the members of moorland parishes the privilege of grazing a certain number of beasts on the open moor, of using the granite, and of collecting peat for fuel. Moormen, appointed to be responsible for every section of the moor, saw to it that these privileges were not abused. Their job was to arrange periodic drifts, which were never announced beforehand, in which all the beasts were rounded up so that their brands could be checked and all strays impounded. At the time when there were still deer in the Royal Forest of Dartmoor, it was the moormen's task to see that no venison got onto the wrong table and that the fuel gatherers did not make away with any branches from living trees.

Dartmoor has been linked with Cornwall from the time that Henry III granted the Forest to his brother, the Earl of Cornwall, as part of his earldom. The combined territories were raised to a duchy by Edward III, who made his son, the Black Prince, the first Duke of Cornwall.

Although it was not until the late twelfth century that any substantial deposits of tin were found on Dartmoor, from that time until the end of the seventeenth century it was the main source of

wealth, 300 tons a year being produced at one period. But even that was much less than the output of Cornwall. By the end of the nineteenth century most of the Devon mines had closed down, although the last mine to be worked, which was near Warren House Inn, went on functioning until 1939.

The laws that governed the mining rights were much more complicated and rigid than those which ordered the grazing rights. Until 1749 the Stannary Parliament for Dartmoor met once a month on Crockern Tor, which was furnished with a stone table and stone seats for the assembly. After that date, although the delegates might start the proceedings on the open moor, they adjourned any lengthy business to a more comfortable meeting place in Tavistock.

Dartmoor too has its share of china clay, that other byproduct of granite. Although once again the workings are not so extensive as those in Cornwall, they are just as dramatic, providing a shining, dead-white landscape, whose only colour comes from sheets of metallic blue water. Here, where nothing lives and only a very few men have to be employed as the clay is mostly extracted by blasting, the scene is weird and inhuman. That effect has been acknowledged by the BBC, who chose the workings at the southwest of the moor for the setting of one episode of 'Dr Who'.

So we come back again to Dartmoor's reputation for being a place where the natural order is constantly being invaded by the supernatural and by the figures of legend. There is only one mention of Arthur on Dartmoor: he is supposed to have emerged victorious from a combat with the devil at Moretonhampstead. Yet Bronze Age monuments and recent quarries alike are haunted by such fabled spirits as the huntsman who rides across the moor with fire-breathing hounds; the pixies or little people; and the witches both living and dead, black and white, who, some will tell you, still hold their covens among the tors.

The fearful huntsman, whom it is death to meet, is not peculiar to Dartmoor, although he appears more frequently here than elsewhere. As for the pixies, as I have already indicated, I hold Margaret Murray's belief (*The God of Witches*, 1931) that they originated in the small Bronze Age men, whose descendants were forced into hiding when the Celts and Saxons settled on the edges of the moor. Like all conquered people, they managed to retain an extraordinary hold on their victors, who constantly felt it necessary to placate them. Baring-Gould reported that a sheep, whose owner was suffering a run of ill fortune, was sacrificed to the pixies as late as 1879, and stories of sightings of the little people are not unknown today.

Although pixie power seems rather unlikely at this date, there is no doubt that some people on Dartmoor, described as 'white witches', are able to cure warts and to stop severe bleeding, and to do this when at some distance from the sufferer. No 'witch' will ever divulge how this power operates except to the single person, usually a member of the opposite sex, who is to inherit the gift.

For myself, I think that most of the stories of evil powers are largely invented by people who have to find some way of confronting the great inhuman force of nature that Dartmoor presents. The way in which an individual's consciousness can shrink from such a confrontation has been well described by Rosalind Heywood in *The Infinite Hive*. Although she is a writer concerned with, and persuaded of, the reality of spiritual beings, her experience of watching a sunset near Okehampton was not of anything unearthly, but of her own littleness in relation to the immense beauty of the moor, which 'towered in shadowed purple contours between us and the sinking sun'.

The prospect gave her the feeling that she 'was no longer looking at Nature. Nature was looking at me. And she did not like what she saw. It was a strange and humbling sensation, as if numberless unoffending creatures were shrinking back offended by our invasion, and it struck me like a blow that even the windswept little tree against the skyline seemed to be leaning away from us in disgust.'

Other visitors to Okehampton throughout the centuries, including the intrepid Celia Fiennes, who was there in 1695, and Daniel Defoe, in 1724, were quite content to make no closer inspection of the moor. The Italian Count Magalotti, in his chronicles of the journey of Cosimo III, Grand Duke of Tuscany, who came to the town in 1669, reported that 'the whole of the country was hilly, with some rather abrupt mountains; some parts were desert'.

Walking across Dartmoor did not become popular until the early years of this century and the publication of William Crossing's *Guide to Dartmoor* in 1912. It is still an undertaking that needs some thought and preparation, but for those with the courage, stamina and experience, or the opportunity of finding a good guide, a long Dartmoor walk is a most exhilarating adventure.

The Bronze Age farmers would not recognize their old settlements, surrounded as they now are by swamps or conifers. In their time broad-leafed trees almost certainly grew at a greater altitude than they do now; and where the bog cotton (locally known as pixie grass from the belief that the little people use it to lure men to their deaths), mosses, lichen and asphodel abound on the quaking heights of the moor, their beasts enjoyed rich grazing. Nor could they have known the profusion of Dartmoor's three types of heather (ling, bell and cross-leaved), interspersed with the startling yellow tormentil, whose boiled roots are said to be a cure for stomachache, and which certainly produce a rich red dye. For these are plants that flourish on the peat.

Today, the marshes and woods of Dartmoor, rich in fungi, ferns and lichens which only grow profusely in pure air, are a botanist's delight. Ornothologists are a little less fortunate. Unlike Exmoor, whose coombes abound with all sorts of birds, the only ones that you are now likely to see on Dartmoor are buzzards, kestrels, wheatears, dippers, pippets and larks.

Although these heights no longer provide much grazing, the local people will tell you that the higher up on the slopes the sheep, cattle and ponies venture in search of food, the better the prospects of the weather being fine. Like Exmoor ponies, the Dartmoor natives are now a rare species. Horses are here in great numbers, but the true Dartmoor pony, bay, brown or black, is hardly ever seen. The herds now are largely made up of brightly coloured chestnut crossbreeds, with an intermingling of skewbald animals.

The cattle, which have to withstand bleak winters, are mainly Scottish breeds, black and belted Galloways making a welcome change from the similarly coloured but less dramatic ubiquitous Friesians of the lowlands. A few years before William Crossing started to write his guide, the wild, shaggy, dun-coloured, long-horned Highland cattle were introduced onto the moor, and a few of these are still to be seen. As for the sheep, they are mostly Scottish too, hardy black-faced animals, occasionally running with some of the white-faced, curly-coated, aristocratic-looking breed which is the true Dartmoor native.

I have described six walks that trace patterns across the landscape of the moor. The first follows the dragon line from East Week near Okehampton to the St Michael's church on the top of Brent Tor; the second goes along the trading routes which have been in use since prehistoric times, and which pass through the Bronze Age settlement of Grimspound; the third takes the so-called Abbots' Way between Buckfast and Tavistock; the fourth follows the coffin bearers, who had to carry their loads across the moor to Lydford where the burials from the Forest of Dartmoor took place; the fifth goes over ground mapped out by Major F. C. Tyler (*The Geometrical Arrangement of Ancient Sites*, 1939), who did some ley hunting on the moor in the 1930s; and the sixth looks at one of Richard Long's landscape sculptures.

Spinsters Rock

Walk 1
The Dragon Path to Land's End

The existence of the so-called dragon path, which runs from Glastonbury Tor to Land's End, and which was once firmly believed to be part of a pattern of ley alignments linking Stonehenge to the far west of Cornwall, is now doubted by many serious investigators of the course of ley energy; they prefer to base their observations on shorter lengths of territory. Nevertheless, it is obvious from the findings of the more academic archaeologists that trade routes existed along this route from Neolithic times and that a straight line drawn on the map between the two places passes through several churches dedicated to Michael the Archangel, who fought the dragon, as well as through many Celtic, Bronze Age and Stone Age sites.

Before embarking on this walk, you can get some idea of the high terrain the dragon line passes over by taking the lane that runs out of the village of Hatherleigh towards Monkokehampton. Stop when you reach the obelisk [191: 555046] put up to commemorate John Henry Thomson, who fell at Balaklava, and look south. The highest land in southern Britain towers up to the horizon from Cawsand Hill in the east to High Willhays in the west. When we come to walk here, we will find that

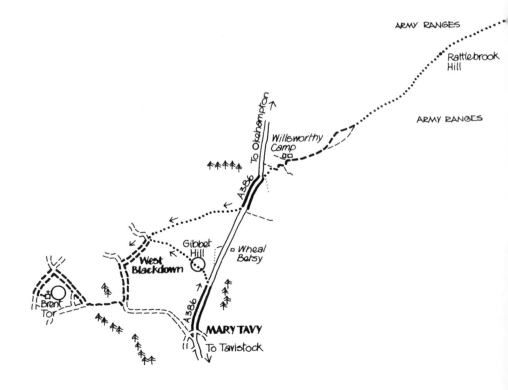

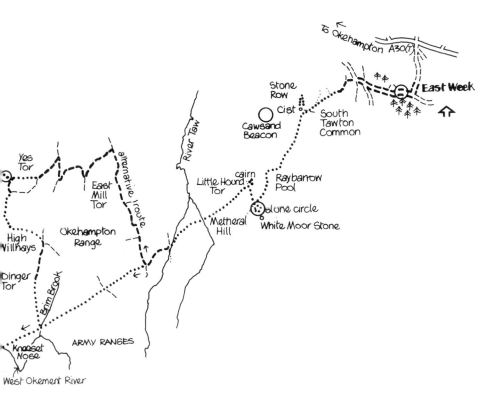

the intersections of these hills are swampy with the headwaters of the Taw and Okement rivers, but at this safe distance it is easy to be allured by the majesty of the high moor.

The dragon line enters the Dartmoor National Park by the village of East Week [191: 665920], where it crosses the old salt road of Devon which goes from Sticklepath through Bovey Tracey to Teignmouth. East Week is simply a straggle of farms and cottages on either side of a narrow lane. To the west the heights of the moor rise steeply, their lower slopes patchworked with intake fields enclosed in stone walls. Turn right when you come to the T junction [191: 654924] at the moor end of the village and almost immediately you will come to a bridle path, which runs first of all along the bottom of these fields between walls interspersed with holly and hazel, the last trees you will see for some time.

The climb up to South Tawton Common starts abruptly from this path, going along a narrow passage between the walls of the fields. When they end, a gate at the top leads through onto the sparse, rough vegetation of the common. This is the real start of the walk along the dragon path. From this point you can look east to the Bronze Age track along the southern ridge of Exmoor, a route that was probably familiar to the people who lived in the hut circles, whose rudimentary remains are still visible here. Probably they also built the stone rows between the common and Cawsand Beacon, whose pagan boulders are supposed to start dancing at the sound of South Tawton church bells.

That village was the home of old Uncle Tom Cobbley and all his friends, who had fourteen miles to go south over the moor to Hameldown before they could revel at Widecombe Fair. They must have started off round the east side of Cosdon or Cosson Hill, which was the original name of the place until the Ordnance Survey dubbed it Cawsand in 1888. It must have been a tough journey for that overladen old grey mare, but perhaps she was able to pick up some energy from the dragon

21

line which runs to the west of Raybarrow Pool, which is no shimmering stretch of water, but one of the most dangerous bogs on Dartmoor. The way they went was also the probable route taken by the first men to perambulate Dartmoor Forest when they set out from Cosdon Hill in 1240.

Do not attempt to cross Raybarrow Pool, but follow the wet peaty path round the mire, which drains a large area of moorland, if you wish to see the seventeen stones of the White Moor Circle [191: 633897] on the saddle between Hound Tor and White Hill, and their outrider, the White Stone, 170 yards to the southeast. To rejoin the dragon path, head north again to the cairn which marks its course.

The invisible path runs on to the southwest over a magnificent peaty wilderness, crossing Metheral Hill, Kneeset Nose and Rattlebrook Hill, where in 1901 unsuccessful attempts were made to carbonize the peat by pressing it between heated plates. The route can generally only be followed in August for the way lies across the army ranges and during the rest of the year shooting can be going on at any time, although there are some clear days. The National Park Information Service has a list of safe times for several weeks ahead. Yet even if you are not threatened by military activity, this walk is full of hazards, so unless you are very experienced indeed, do not attempt it without a companion who knows the moor well. I have not been this way myself, but I am assured that it can be done. If you make this walk, then should you also make the diversion along the track going north over Okehampton Range to Yes Tor [191: 580903], whose summit is marked by a double prehistoric enclosure, explored by Baring-Gould in 1898. From Yes Tor the alignment can be rejoined by taking the route over High Willhays, the highest point of the moor.

Those who decide, as I did, to leave the dragon path at Little Hound Tor can take up its story at the western edge of the moor, starting at Mary Tavy, where William Crossing and his wife Emma made their final home. Just north of the village is the Wheal Betsy, the remains of an old silver and lead mine, surrounded by some of the nineteenth-century copper workings in this area, a stretch of industrial archaeology which is now owned and maintained by the National Trust. Running close by it is the Reddaford leat, which was originally cut to supply water for this mine and the other copper workings of Wheal Jewell and Wheal Friendship.

On the other side of the road from the mine workings a footpath goes over Gibbet Hill [191: 503813], the supposed site of the burning of the notorious Lady Howard. According to Crossing, this was also the place where the unfortunate wretches, some of whom may have been her victims, were confined in an iron cage. The lady, who was said to have been convicted of witchcraft, lived near Tavistock in the seventeenth century. She was married four times and inherited large fortunes from her first three husbands, all of whom died in a dubious manner, probably by poison. Certainly the portrait that Van Dyke painted of the lady shows an expression of implacable arrogance which makes it quite believable that this would be the sort of person to grasp power and money at all costs to those about her and then use it to tyrannize the rest of her neighbours.

However, that is a case of prejudice being reinforced by legend, for in fact Mary Fitz, the wealthy Devon heiress who died as Lady Howard, was married for the third time before she was sixteen, and was certainly a victim rather than an instigator of greedy contrivances. Her fourth husband, Sir Richard Grenville, a dependant of the Duke of Buckingham, treated her exceedingly badly, took control of her Devon home of Fitzford and installed his aunt as housekeeper. Which explains why she chose to keep the name of Howard, her third husband, and does a little to exonerate her cruelty to her daughters Elizabeth and Mary Grenville.

It was that behaviour which got her so disliked in her lifetime that after her death the tale grew up that her ghost was doomed to be constantly on the move between Tavistock and Okehampton Castle, where she was compelled to pluck a single blade of grass on each visit and carry it home in her mouth. Her torment will only come to an end when all the grass is cleared. Meanwhile she rides along that stretch of the moor in a coach which also carries the skulls of her husbands, preceded by a ghostly black dog, whose one eye in the centre of its forehead stares at the terrified passers-by. Frightening as the creature must be, it is only one of the many phantom black dogs that have been reported on this part of the moor. Some say that this particular black dog is Lady Howard herself, and that the coach with the rattling skulls is driven by a headless coachman along the lanes around West Blackdown.

The walk goes along that haunted way, the route dominated by the 1100-foot-high volcanic outcrop of Brent Tor [191: 471805], surmounted by the thirteenth-century church of St Michael de Rupe. The final climb has to be made from the west side of the hill, through the defences of an Iron Age fort whose banks, bright in summer with blue sheep's bit scabeous, red betony and yellow tormentil, were used throughout the Middle Ages as fortified enclosures for the abbey lands.

The church itself, in a tradition endorsed by Charles Kingsley in *Westward Ho!*, is said to have been built by a merchant landowner, generally named as Robert Giffard, who, being shipwrecked during the course of a tremendous storm, vowed to St Michael that if he survived he would build a church on the first land he saw. Whether that is so or not, this church has served for centuries as a landmark for sailors coming into Plymouth, and for us it is a pointer towards the next moorland part of the dragon path, which crosses the south of Bodmin Moor.

Walk 2
Bronze Age Tracks

The Bronze Age village of Grimspound lies in the narrow valley between King Tor and Hameldown, on the eastern edge of the moor, in an area that was then heavily populated and extensively farmed. This walk visits the remains of that village, and follows the course of some of the tracks that must have been familiar to the people who lived there.

The walk starts at Manaton church [191: 749804], and if you happen to be doing it on a Thursday in summer, you may find the weekly charity stall on the village green quite useful. There you can buy a little provender for your walk; or if, like me, you have foolishly come out on a cold day with no head covering – and Hameldown can be very chilly even in high summer – that can be quickly and cheaply remedied by the purchase of a knitted wool cap. The lane from Manaton leads to the footpath for Hayne Down, from whose heights the right-hand profile of Bowerman's Nose is clearly visible. Many prehistorians consider that this impressive rock must have been taken as a god by the Bronze Age dwellers on these downs, and early antiquarians even thought that it was shaped by Druids. But it is a purely natural quirk, and its name is simply a corruption of the Celtic *vawr-maen*, the great stone.

To the west of Cripdon Down, the footpath, which is bounded by a stone wall, makes a cross with the lane [191: 733799]. In the northwest corner of this cross, a simple grave marks one of Dartmoor's saddest stories. The mound is kept fresh throughout the year with flowers, yellow ones being chosen whenever the season permits. They stand in a simple jamjar, and no one is allowed to know who puts them there. 'The pixies do it,' said my no-nonsense cousin from Manaton, when I had hoped that family ties might persuade her to divulge the mystery. All that you and I are allowed to know is that the custom was started by Beatrice Chase of Widecombe in the first part of this century. No one will tell how it has been perpetuated since she died.

Underneath the flowers lie the remains of Kitty Jay, an orphan in an eighteenth-century poor house, who was seduced at the age of sixteen by a labourer employed on the farm where she drudged. This happened at a time when pregnancy out of wedlock was an unforgivable crime, so when the poor girl discovered her condition, without even waiting to know her fate, she hanged herself in one of the barns. The righteous were no kinder to the dead than they were to the living. As a suicide, no churchyard would give her room, and so she was buried at the spot where the three parishes of Manaton, North Bovey and Widecombe meet.

John Galsworthy, who lived for some time in the neighbourhood, wove this grave into a story of his own. In *The Apple Tree* he turns Kitty Jay into a poor Welsh girl, Megan David, who is seduced and betrayed by a young Edwardian 'masher', who thinks better of his promise to elope with her. I find a better literary outcome to the real Kitty's tragedy in the verses of Margaret Calloway, a more recent poet who knew Dartmoor well. In 'The Moor's Geometry' (*Jay's Grave*, Grael Communications, Torquay, n.d.), she imagines that this suicide, whose 'life's circumference' was measured by a loop of rope, was aware of being encompassed by the ancient lines of the moor:

> My cold green days surrounded
> By lines and by perimeters. Life curled
> In cairns, huts, pounds. My granite hours
> bounded
> By stone rows.

Whoever was the cause of Kitty's taking her life

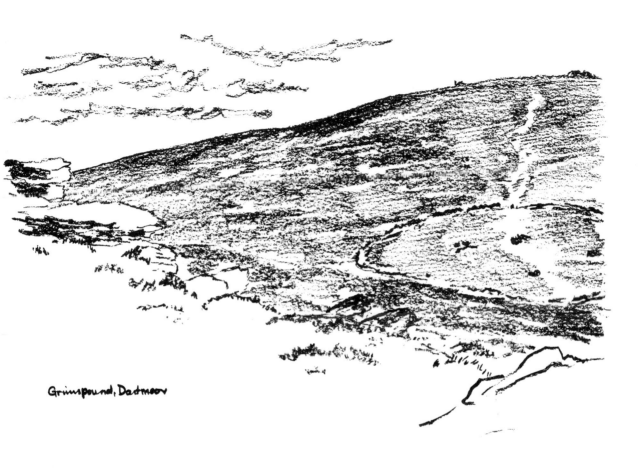

Grimspound, Dartmoor

may have known of it and felt remorse, for a strange ghost has been seen at these crossroads. Several travellers have reported seeing a man draped in a blanket standing by the grave. No face appears among the folds, and no feet stand on the ground.

West from the grave, a grassy track goes to Natsworthy Gate, and from there it is possible to go directly onto the open country of Hameldown, but, for the purpose of following the trackways round the Bronze Age settlements, it is best to turn right and go north along the lane by Natsworthy Manor. This lane, which continues as a footpath through the conifer plantation by the manor, is a part of the Mariners' Way, which ran between the south and north coasts of Devon. Its name comes from the sailors who walked along it on their way to look for work on new ships. This walk leaves the Mariners' Way before it goes into the wood and joins the path [191: 721803] which climbs westwards to the north of Berry Pound, and on to the village of Grimspound itself.

The enclosure that surrounds this village contains the remains of twenty-four huts, once the homes of the people who farmed here from the middle of the fourth century BC. The dwellings and the cattle kraal which probably stood among them were protected by a wall which archaeologists reckon must have been even thicker than it was high; the measurement through it is some 9 feet, and it is thought to have stood 6 feet tall. Most of the stones marking the doorways of the remains of the huts within it face to the south, away from the prevailing winds; in the centre of each hut is the stone that supported the main roof pole, and in many of them the raised stone platform that served as a bed can still be seen. The home of the chief man of the village differs from the others simply by its larger size and by its double entrance way.

The people who lived here knew the secrets of Dartmoor's stone rows, whose mystery is even more intractable than that of the flowers on Kitty Jay's grave. Whatever rites were conducted at the stone rows, they cannot have been more cruel than the pressures that drove Kitty Jay to suicide. In order to make a living out of their primitive agriculture the people who lived here must have been both peaceful and industrious. That their village should have attracted the name of Grim is a historical accident. Grim, with its reference to the Devil, or to Odin in his most fearful aspects, was connected with the ruins by the Anglo-Saxons. They feared all old dwellings of conquered peoples, whose ghosts were thought to linger round them.

The walk leaves Grimspound by its imposing southern entrance and climbs up to the 1700-feet height of Hameldown. The length of the ridgeway running south is marked by cairns and barrows. In one of these a Bronze Age dagger was found, inlaid with gold and amber, that precious substance whose changing colours were thought to indicate that it had living and magical powers. Perhaps this vital talisman came from Scandinavia, although a little of this fossilized conifer gum was to be found in southeast England at that time. In any case, whoever brought it to this place had travelled some distance, and some of his journey would have been along the tracks that this walk follows.

The ridgeway runs on towards Widecombe, a village best avoided on the second Tuesday in September, when the famous fair brings cars in their thousands to jam the lanes around it; it is astonishing how many lanes converge here. They have done so since 1260, when Widecombe's church,

dedicated to St Pancras, was first licensed for baptisms and funerals. Until that date, everyone who died on Dartmoor had to be carried northwest to Lydford for burial. The fourth walk in this section covers the way those coffin bearers had to take.

The church, whose great tower has caused it to be known as the cathedral of the moor, is supposed to have been built by local tinners. That assumption was made because, like several other moorland churches, the tinners' device of three rabbits arranged in a triangle is embossed on the roof. But whoever built the church, it was nearly destroyed on Sunday, 21 October 1636, when a great thunderstorm raged overhead just as the Reverend George Lyde had begun his sermon. The story of that fearful event has been written on a board which now hangs in the church. It has been further adorned with some commemorative verses on the fatal storm, written by the village schoolmaster who was present at the time.

That seventeenth-century thunderstorm was to add to the many legends which associate Dartmoor with the Devil. According to the version that William Crossing passed on, the Devil actually conjured up the storm, and he did so because he wanted the soul of Jan Reynolds, who had been foolish enough to enter into a compact with the fiend by the cairn that was built on Blackslade Down [191: 734755], nearby the present Youth Hostel. When the seven years were up and the Devil came to claim his own, he found the unfortunate and unsuspecting Jan dozing through the sermon, clutching a pack of cards in the hopes of finding a mate to play with him as soon as the service was over.

In this state, Jan, his cards still in his hand, was snatched up by the Devil from beneath the parson's very nose, and carried off on the satanic black steed to the tin mines around Warren House Inn. There he dropped the four aces from his pack and they made a substantial mark on the landscape; even now, although the walls have partly collapsed, you can see the outlines of four intakes – new fields made from the moor – each one shaped like one of the suits. They show up best in winter, when the walls surrounding them stand out sharply from the dead bracken and heather.

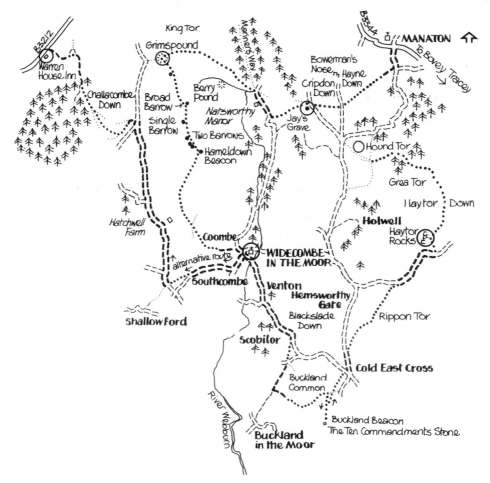

From Widecombe you can either follow the Devil's route, going by the lanes and forestry footpaths to the northwest; or take a longer and initially more holy way by crossing the Walkham river and following the lane that goes southeast to Buckland in the Moor, and then climbing Buckland Beacon [191: 735733] which stands over 1000 feet above the Dart valley. Here, by order of Mr Whitley, a former Lord of the Manor of Buckland, the Ten Commandments were inscribed in the granite.

From the beacon it is possible to return to Manaton by a route that leads through other places, deserted now, which once played a busy part in the life of the moor. The northeast descent from the beacon goes to Cold East Cross, and from there a path climbs up to Rippon Tor [191: 745755] and across to the lane in front of Haytor Rocks. North of these twin pinnacles the ground drops down to the old granite quarries which supplied the stone for that London Bridge which now stands in the desert of Arizona. Here too are the remains of the old tramway along which the stone was carried.

North again from these industrial workings, the moor bears evidence of intense cultivation from the Bronze Age to medieval times. And having started this walk at the Bronze Age village of Grimspound, it is perhaps proper to end it on the fourteenth-century farmland which was cultivated beneath the impressive rocks of Hound Tor, although that means a difficult walk across open moorland by Greator Rocks [191: 753789], or a circuitous journey along the lanes going through Hemsworthy Gate and Holwell.

Walk 3
The Abbots' Way

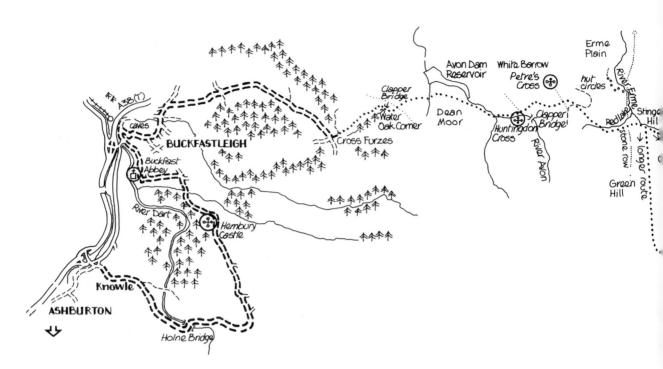

The route between Buckfast Abbey and Whit-church Priory on the outskirts of Tavistock, which we are going to follow on this walk, was given the name of the Abbots' Way in the eighteenth century. It was also more accurately and popularly known as the Jobbers' Way, for it was greatly used by the packmen responsible for the carriage of wool. Although they were mostly on monastic business – both institutions were involved in the wool trade – the route itself was never used exclusively for ecclesiastical purposes. It is simply the driest way across the bogs of southern Dartmoor; the barrows, standing stones and early crosses show that it was well used long before the religious houses came to their prime in the early Middle Ages. There is evidence, too, to show that the tinners and traders of all sorts made great use of it

after that time, so it seems fitting that a walk along it should start from the Stannary town of Ashburton, which stands on the main route from Exeter to Land's End, and which for many years drew its wealth from the making of serge cloth.

This town, which is now almost completely swamped by the large housing estates on its eastern flank, has a centre that retains much of its old character. Here you will find a small museum, which a much-travelled citizen of the town has unexpectedly filled with objects from the Indian cultures of North America; an excellent and roomy secondhand bookshop; and several small galleries and genuine craft shops. They are all housed in buildings which either date from, or are well in keeping with, the years when the whole life of the town was centred on the moor and before it became a place beside a major trunk road.

Although Ashburton did not receive official Stannary status until 1360, the miners brought tin here for weighing and stamping long before that date; it had a flourishing market from the twelfth century. The great St Lawrence Fair, briefly revived in 1952, was first established here in 1310.

There are two ways from this town to the abbey of Buckfast; one goes directly along the lanes parallel to the A38; the other makes a long and beautiful detour through the woods on the western bank of the Dart. It goes past one of the most important archaeological sites in Devon, the Iron Age hill fort of Hembury Castle [202: 726684]. These earthworks were constructed on top of a Neolithic causewayed camp of the fourth millennium BC. The Celtic finds from Hembury are now in the museum at Exeter, and these, together with the conclusions drawn by the excavators of the site, show that a very sophisticated community lived here in buildings linked by cobbled streets. It is in a strategic place above the Dart and must always have been used as a defence post as well as serving as a settlement. Its two functions come together in

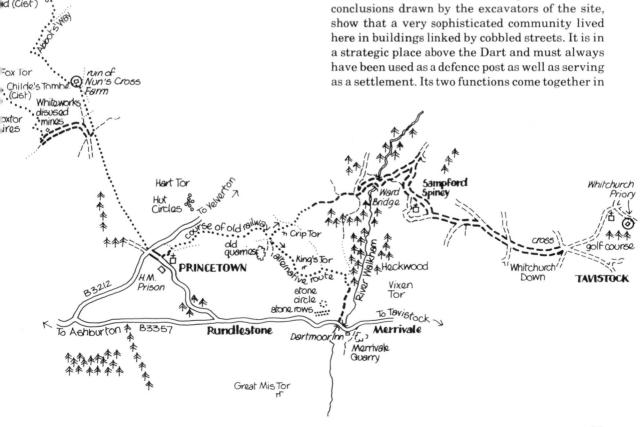

Walk 3   The Abbot's Way

a story related by the Dartmoor folklorist, Theo Brown ('The Folklore of Devon', *Journal of the Folklore Society*, 1964). She records the tradition that when the fort was used as a defence position in some skirmish of historic times, it was guarded solely by women who 'welcomed the enemy, took them to their beds, and stabbed them all in the night'.

From the secular fort of Hembury, the lane goes down to Buckfast Abbey, which stands on a religious site founded in the early years of the eleventh century, when it was endowed by King Canute. The present abbey church, which was built by French Benedictines in 1882, is now at the centre of a tourist industry of almost unrivalled vulgarity, as independent traders muscle in on the genuine work of the monks, who sell their produce here and who are most noted for their rich Dartmoor honey. Now, the only peace to be found in the place emanates from the humble kitchen gardens of the late nineteenth-century Methodist church, which stands opposite the abbey gateway, and from the two ruined crosses in the flowerbeds by the abbey car park.

The walk across the open moor starts at Cross Furzes [202: 700667], reached by the lanes going through Buckfastleigh, whose wool mills were engaged in the production of serge and blankets until the beginning of this century. Now it is particularly worth visiting for the Pengelly Caves Study Centre [202: 744663], which owns the five caves in the limestone here, and which is the only institution in Britain to concentrate solely on cave research. The entrance to it is at the top of Russetts Lane, between the Dart Bridge and the railway station. The caves open onto an overgrown, disused quarry, which is now a nature reserve, and the whole area contains a mixture of extinct and living wild life. The interior of these caves bear evidence both of the very early people, and of the long-vanished species of animals which found shelter in these cliffs. They also provide an almost unrivalled opportunity for studying the differing species and habits of late-twentieth-century bats, whose reputation as enemies of mankind is most ill-deserved. Certainly they have never done anything like the amount of harm perpetuated by tyrannical squires, such as the man who is supposed to have been buried in the churchyard above the caves with a lump of limestone on his chest to ensure that he did not get up and continue his bullying ways. The story goes that as he was unable to go up, he went down; in the cave beneath the churchyard there is a piece of stone in the shape of a fossilized person known as 'the little man'.

The lanes through Buckfastleigh, with its early music centre housed in the old chapel, lead up to the heath of Cross Furzes and the bridlepath, which carries a sign directing walkers to the Abbots' Way. This path runs through a small wood and across an ancient clapper bridge [202: 698665]. From there it starts to climb through agricultural land onto the open moor. The route here is marked by posts and, in order to disturb the land as little as possible, it is considerate to keep close to these and to walk in single file. This route goes through fields that have been established for many centuries. The divisions between them are still marked by some of the original boundary reaves, banks made of earth and stone, which are happily being restored as the cost of barbed wire soars.

The open moor starts at Water Oak Corner [202: 689661], from where the water of the moor is pumped down to Buckfastleigh. Looking west from the ridge above this point, you can see the conical cairn of White Barrows and, farther south along the skyline, the three barrows of Ugborough Beacon, where a fire was lit at the time of the Armada and more recently for the Queen's Jubilee. Another odder reminder of recent history stands in the wooden posts that dot these moors. They are the very opposite of waymarkers, having been put up to stop German gliders landing here during the last war. To get them in place, local men were employed at sixpence a head to spend one Sunday afternoon at the work.

This particular stretch of the moor was familiar to the poet Herrick, who was the reluctant vicar of Dean Prior from 1629, when he was thirty-eight, to his death at the age of eighty-three. The place was a hated wilderness to him, for he regarded his appointment as exile and longed for London. But even in his time this part of the moor was not as desolate as it is today and there are signs that the valley at the head of the river Avon was extensively settled during the Bronze Age.

From the ridge, this walk goes down to that valley, reaching it by the marshes that lie above the Avon Dam Reservoir. On the southern tip of Dean Moor, to the left of the path that goes towards Huntingdon Cross, there is a Bronze Age burial cairn [202: 678654] made up of a circular stone ring surrounding a granite cist. On the hillside on the other side of the path are the remains of the Bronze Age village where the buried chieftain may once have lived when he ordered the working of these lands.

Although this remote hillside encampment is less orderly than the much visited Grimspound, the circular banks on the rough slope contain evidence of a settlement that must once have been of equal importance. The stones which indicate the remains of the huts here show that each one was protected by a double wall infilled with earth; they were so sited that each dwelling had its own water supply channelled from the Avon. Three of the huts still have interior stone divisions indicating separate sleeping quarters, and it is likely that this arrangement was common to them all.

The people who lived here were probably the first tinners on the moor, for pebbles of tin ore and blobs of tin slag discovered below the settlement have been given a prehistoric dating. But whether the original dwellers were tinners or not, they were certainly farmers. As at Grimspound, the circular earthwork which surrounds the remains of the huts marked out a cattle kraal as well as a human village. More Bronze Age enclosures stand to the north of Huntingdon Cross, and on the hill above them a single sycamore tree marks the

Hut-circle, Dartmoor

Dartmoor Clapper bridge

remains of a more recent venture, North Huntingdon Warren. All round this part of the moor are signs of the tinners who worked here and poached rabbits in their spare time. In doing so they ran a constant battle with the resident gamekeeper, warfare which probably continued in the two pubs which once stood nearby on the banks of the Avon. The place was still occupied in the nineteenth century, for when the naturalist, Keble-Martin, camped at the farm which then stood at Huntingdon Warren, the land of this hill supported a family whose children daily walked 3 miles to school at Scorriton.

The Abbots' Way crosses the clapper bridge over the Avon and then goes due west along the slopes of the hill below White Barrows to the height of Petre's Cross [202: 654655] and on towards the swamps around Red Lake. Before it reaches that marsh, it meets another route [202: 646659] which goes south over Ugborough Moor to Ivybridge.

That is another section of the Abbots' Way and runs from Tavistock towards the Augustinian Priory of Plympton St Mary, founded on the site of a Saxon monastery on the outskirts of Plymouth. That route is followed in the course of Walk 5.

To the west of that track is an even more ancient north–south mark on the moor's surface, made by the long stone row which runs from Green Hill to the stone circle on Erme Plains. If you follow it south along the banks of the river, you will come to groups of Bronze Age hut circles, some of which have been rebuilt into cattle pounds [202: 641654] for the empounding of those beasts whose owners did not hold moorland grazing rights, and for sorting and rebranding the herds of those who did. Crossing suggests that the drovers managing these drifts of cattle used the ruins of the building outside Erme Pound itself as a shelter, and that that is why there are signs of a stone bench round its inner wall.

Just past Red Lake, at the foot of Stinger's Hill, the way divides again [202: 633664]. From here one path goes north past Fox Tor and Childe's Tomb; the other takes the slightly easier way by Nun's Cross Farm. That second route starts across the swamp of Erme Head, which has to be negotiated with some care. From the top of Great Gnats' Head, to the west of the swamp, the Abbots' Way zigzags towards Nun's Cross Farm.

The cross which gave the hill farm its name stands a little to the west of it, a great pillar over 7 feet high and measuring nearly 3 feet across the arms. The shaft was broken in 1846 by two lads who were out looking for cattle across the moor and were apparently driven to vandalism by the frustration they found in that activity.

Despite various short-lived attempts to grow flax and hemp in the vicinity of Princetown, farming on Dartmoor, in common with hill farming in general, has always been largely a matter of rearing and grazing stock and herding sheep. There are no pastures suitable for large dairy undertakings, or fit for arable cultivation. This means that much of a farmer's work still consists in making certain of the whereabouts of his own branded animals, and in seeing that they have enough to eat in winter. Such work can be cold, lonely and tedious, and those of us who walk on the moor in summer for interest and delight need not be too harsh on the shades of those lads, who found the familiar place an empty desert which they could only confront by some act of destruction.

There are no nuns associated with the cross, for the farm's name comes from the Celtic *nante*, a valley, and these lands were first enclosed around 1870. The cross itself is very much older. It is marked with the name of Siward, and it is as Siward's Cross that it is marked on ancient charters showing the boundaries of Dartmoor Forest, and mentioned in a perambulation of the moor made in 1240. Siward himself was an earl of Northumberland who was granted estates on the western edge of Dartmoor by William the Conqueror. From his stone the Abbots' Way runs north-northwest above the lane from Whiteworks.

The longer route to this point goes along the western slopes of Green Hill, following the course of Black Lane, a peat cutters' track, which made use of the natural pass from Stinger's Hill to Fox Tor, between the marshes round the head of the Plym to the west and those of the Avon to the east. At the southern edge of the marsh, round the head of the Plym, you will find Duck's Pool [202: 624679], which boasts one of Dartmoor's letterboxes. These are simple tin containers with a rubber stamp inside for walkers to record their journeys across the moor. Of more historic interest are the remains of old tin streamings and the blowing house that served them, as well as the small bronze memorial tablet for William Crossing.

From here the walk goes over Fox Tor, where four hundred years ago a certain Childe, who owned much land at Plymstock, is said to have lost his way while out hunting. He was caught in a blizzard and, freezing to death, he attempted to save his life by killing his horse and climbing into the still-warm carcass. His efforts failed, but just before he died he wrote his will in the horse's blood. It was to the effect that whoever should bury his body should inherit his lands. When this awful document was discovered, the men of Plymstock and Tavistock raced for the prize. The latter won by taking an unexpected route across the moor.

For many years a memorial stone to Childe's memory stood under Fox Tor, and according to Tristram Risdon's seventeenth-century *Survey of Devon*, it bore the inscription:

> They fyrste that fyndes and brings mee to my grave
> The priories of Plimstoke they shall have.

But the monument was destroyed in 1812 by a Mr Windeath, who used part of its stone in the building of Fox Tor Farm. The late-nineteenth-century monument which now stands on a piece of ground known as Sands Park is close by a Bronze Age cist. This monument, still popularly known as Childe's Tomb, lies to the right of the path which goes round Foxtor Mires to the disused mines of Whiteworks [202: 613710].

These mines, which were still in operation about a hundred years ago, were known to

Crossing as a young man. He recorded that they were owned by Mr Moses Bawden of Tavistock, who had set up several similar enterprises throughout the moor. Crossing could remember the time 'when two large waterwheels were seen to be revolving here, and when the blacksmith's hammer was constantly heard ringing on the anvil.' But by 1912, when he published his famous guide to the moor, the mine was closed down and the scattered people had turned again to stock farming as a means of livelihood.

From Whiteworks, a lane joins the main track of the Abbots' Way as it runs over South Hessary Tor to Princetown. Before you reach that grim settlement, it is worth taking a slight detour to the west and looking at the hut circles beneath the twin rock towers of Hart Tor [191: 584724]. The straight descent from that point brings you out on the Yelverton road into Princetown, at a place marked as the Devil's Elbow on the map and known to Crossing as the Devil's Bridge. As he says, there is no tale to be told about this name. It simply refers to the man who built the culverts which serve the nearby smelting place and blowing house, and who was known at least to his mates as 'Devil'. It does, however, set the tone for the settlement to the north of it.

Princetown was first established in 1806 as a place of custody for the Frenchmen who were captured during the Napoleonic wars. It was these prisoners who built Princetown church, and whose labour was used to dig and clear several of the leats that drain the moor. Although Murray's 1859 *Handbook for Devon and Cornwall* praises the prison building for the way all its arrangements were 'contrived with every regard to the comfort and health of the inmates for whom the building was intended', the prisoners failed to show a proper gratitude for their situation. A. M. Catel, a more contemporary writer, was probably nearer the mark when he complained: 'For seven months in the year it is a *vraie Sibérie* covered with melting snow. When the snows go away the mists appear. Imagine the tyranny of perfide Albion in sending human beings to such a place.'

When the French wars were over, the prison was used for a short time as a base for business enterprises engaged in extracting naphtha from the peat. But the venture was not successful and in 1850 the buildings were once more used as a penal settlement, and so they have remained. The prisoners have always been made to work on the land. In 1852, the value of the labour of the 1051 convicts housed there in producing crops which included flax as well as corn and vegetables was estimated at £13,000. That was not the only contribution they made, for Murray's *Handbook* also notes that: 'For the improvement of the land the sewage is collected, and forced into an elevated tank, from which it is distributed over the fields.'

Princetown, which had been planned as the capital of a restored and thriving landscape, is a miserable place now, especially in summer when hordes of rubber-necking tourists drive slowly past the prison gates. If you follow their course you will come to the first main road across the moor, built in 1722, some sixty years before Thomas Tyrwhitt, secretary to the Prince of Wales and Lord Warden of the Stannaries, started his plan for reclamation. He built his main farm at Tor Royal, calling the settlement after his royal master, set up an inn there to be known as 'The Plume of Feathers' and by the accident of the Napoleonic wars was largely responsible for establishing the penal colony.

The 7-foot-high Rundlestone marks the point where the two roads join. It stands roughly halfway between South Hessary Tor and Great Mis Tor. The main road links Moretonhampstead and Tavistock, but this walk goes to the west by a more southerly route, crossing a track built by French prisoners and following the course of the old Princetown railway.

The railway grew out of the tram road which Tyrwhitt started in order to facilitate the naphtha business and to further his schemes for making Princetown the thriving centre of the moor. In its early days it ran for 20 miles across open country, the wagons being drawn by horses, which are said to have been stabled in the building now used as a toolshed for the Yelverton golf course. The first steam train went along the lines in 1882, and the railway provided one of the most beautiful train journeys in Britain until it fell victim to the

Vixen Tor

Beeching axe in 1958. At the height of its importance, it served the disused quarry of Foggin Tor, which lies a little to the north of it, linked to the line by its own stone tramway. This quarry was blasted out of the granite by gunpowder from the mill at Postbridge, and its stone was used in the construction of Nelson's Monument in Trafalgar Square. No doubt everyone found it fitting enough that the French prisoners should have been instrumental in getting it on its way to London.

Like all disused quarries, this one is a mixture of romance and horror, with its flooded pits and great ruined buildings, which include a smelting shed once fired with peat. A hundred years ago this was an active, busy place; now it is inhabited by occasional ponies, Scottish belted Galloways – which are hardy enough to withstand the cold winters of this southern moor – and foxes who are not scared of running here in broad daylight.

There are two ways of concluding this walk. The first follows the course of the old railway to the west of King's Tor, and then takes the path north through Heckwood. The growth of stunted oaks here, with their delicate covering of ferns and lichens, is almost as old as that at Wistman's Wood (see page 38). The path runs beneath the low hill of Vixen Tor [191: 543744], whose summit carries the tall, oddly shaped granite stack from which it gets its name, and which earns it its place as the highest tor on the moor; the word 'tor' simply refers to the projecting rock.

The path comes out at the main road opposite Merrivale Quarry, the only one of the old quarries on the moor still in operation, and the Dartmoor Inn [191: 548753]. Uphill from there and a little to the southeast, there is the most accessible group of Bronze Age antiquities on the moor. They include a tall menhir and a sacred circle of small stones which at one time enclosed a cairn, situated on a piece of level ground, at the end of a double stone row. Other stones in this complex have a more recent history. One is called the Potato Market or

Walk 3 The Abbot's Way

the Plague Market, from the time when goods, including potatoes, were brought here for sale while the plague was raging in Tavistock. And by the roadside there is a large granite quern or cider press, abandoned perhaps when its maker realized that the farmer who had ordered it was never going to pay up.

The second route comes nearer to the Abbots' Way which runs farther south. It goes across Criptor towards the lanes that lead to Whitchurch, where travellers were able to rest before setting out on the last stages of their journey to Tavistock Abbey. We follow it by crossing the river Walkham at Ward Bridge, and going through Sampford Spiney, past the kennels to Whitchurch Down. Incorporated into one of the walls that stand to the south of this lane there is an ancient blowing stone, a block with a concave edge. To make a sound that could be heard for many miles over the moor, a horn was blown against this depression to cause an ear-splintering and resounding echo. The noise was used to summon tenant farmers to help with the rounding up of stock. However, this is unfortunately still hearsay to me, for I have yet to recognize this stone among the granite boulders that make up these walls.

At the western end of the downs, the lanes form a crossroads, marked by an old milestone, a cross and a boundary stone. The latter has the letter W on one side of it and a T on the other. They stand for Whitchurch and Tavistock, both of which places are about a mile away.

Stone row, Merrivale

Walk 4
The Lich Path

Until the late thirteenth century, everyone who died within the bounds of the Forest of Dartmoor had to be taken to Lydford for burial. That meant that coffins from the farms in the east had to be carried along a 'lich path', or road of the dead, which stretched the whole width of the moor. The actual route that the bearers took varied slightly according to the weather, and was never a single definite track. So although the families in the east, who argued for the law to be changed so that burials could also take place at Widecombe, claiming that Lydford church was 8 miles away when the weather was fair but 15 when it was stormy, were speaking subjectively, it is certainly objectively true that in bad weather lengthy diversions had to be made.

Now, although various paths across the moor are known as the Lich Path, there is no obvious connected route; and like the Abbots' Way, many of the tracks, which follow the driest course through the bogs, were also used by the tinners. A serious hazard for anyone trying to follow these routes now is the army training ground, which occupies most of the northwest of Dartmoor. If you want to complete this full walk, you have to do it in August, which is always a clear month, or at some time when you can be sure that firing is not taking place (see page 22).

It might seem appropriate for this walk to start at the Coffin Stone [191: 678734], which lies beside the main road to the east of Dartmeet; but the stone is outside the forest bound and so could never have been part of the lich path to Lydford. In any case, it probably dates from after 1260, when the Bishop of Exeter decreed funerals on the eastern edge of the moor could take place at Widecombe, so any coffin that rested on it would have been bound for that village rather than Lydford. The stone consists of two granite slabs (recogniz-able among all the clutter of granite beside the road) which are supposed to have split apart when the corpse of a particularly wicked man was laid on top of them.

In any case, despite the associations of the Coffin Stone, the Forest Inn at Hexworthy [191: 653726] makes a more cheerful and interesting start to the first part of this walk, which goes along the eastern boundary of the forest. Crossing claimed that the best view of Dartmoor was to be had from the door of this inn, which was once kept by his friend Richard Cleave. From here on the north side of the lane to Huccaby, before the bridge across the West Dart, the Jolly Lane Cot still stands. It is the last house to have been built on Dartmoor in a day. Tom Satterley, ostler at the inn at Two Bridges, built it in 1832, at midsummer, for his eighteen-year-old bride Sally. In doing so, he made use of the ancient law that gave anyone who could build a house on common land in one day the right to live in it for ever. It is a happy story: Sally lived to a ripe old age, and as Granny Satterley she became the source of much of Baring-Gould's Dartmoor song collection. 'Widecombe Fair' was one of the tunes he got from her. Her old home is a solid stone cottage, which looks as though it will withstand several more centuries of Dartmoor winters.

From the Jolly Lane Cot, a path climbs west-wards onto the moor to join the track that leads from the old mine workings to the bank of the Swincombe river. This walk follows the western bank of that river northwards until it joins the West Dart, and then continues to the main road and Dunnabridge Pound [191: 646746]. Like many others on the moor, this pound was built on the site of an old settlement and cattle kraal. Its entrance is marked by a large stone which is believed to have Bronze Age origins, although the local story is that it was once part of the furniture from the Stannary Parliament on Crockern Tor, and for this reason it is generally known as the Judge's Seat. Another, more authentic, relic from that parliament is the tinners' stone table, which is now at Dunnabridge Farm to the south.

The track goes northeast to Lough or Laughter Tor, whose name is simply another example of the Dartmoor practice of incorporating the word 'tor' into the main name of a hill and then adding a second 'tor'. From here the path through the forest descends to the East Dart and follows its west bank as far as the lane that leads to the Youth Hostel at Bellever. On the way it goes past the ruins of a house which Crossing knew as White Slade, but which is generally known as Snaily House. Two old women are supposed to have lived and flourished here on a diet of slugs and snails preserved in salt. Their story has recently been told in verse by Gillian Stone (*Snaily House*, Dartington Books of Poetry No. 2, 1978), who describes how the two women mystified the villagers by their sleek and healthy appearance although they were never seen to take any food into the house or to grow any food and vegetables in the garden. The rumour got about that they were witches, and when ten men broke into the house to apprehend them, they found the rooms completely bare. The women had wisely walked on the moor, leaving behind them 'three black pickling pots of earthenware' full of 'snails and fat black slugs'.

At the lane by the modern houses put up by the Forestry Commission at Bellever, the ways part. I shall take the more southerly of the two conjectured coffin roads first, for it follows the more clearly defined path. It starts off by going west past a stone cist and a group of hut circles to join the road south of Postbridge. There is a gate immediately across that road leading to a marshy field and the clapper bridge that crosses Cherry Brook near the tall chimney of Powder Mills Farm [191: 628769], all that remains of a gunpowder enterprise started in 1844. Unfortunately, although this path was obviously part of the old route, and is indeed marked as a footpath on the Ordnance Survey map, it is no longer a right of way. So instead of going that way to Wistman's Wood, you must take the road to Two Bridges past Crockern Tor, and then take the footpath that leads out of the car park [191: 609750]. It runs just above the east bank of the West Dart, and brings you to the most famous and most haunted wood on the moor. Some of the stunted trees here, whose roots have to find nourishment through a few inches of top soil over the granite, are at least six hundred years old. Although this little wood, standing on its pile of rocks, has now been classified as a nature reserve, its ghosts are not entirely exorcised. They get life from the grotesque appearance of the wizened trees themselves, and from the fact that the place was long acclaimed as a sacred site.

It is very unlikely however that the druids ever had anything to do with this wood, for the Celts, like the Romans, seem to have given Dartmoor a wide berth. Perhaps it was the Saxons, who made their farms on the outskirts of the moor, who first thought of the wood as the home of Odin and his wild hunt, for it is derivatives of that story which primarily haunt the place. Although the compilers of Murray's *Handbook* believed that the name of the wood came from 'Woods of the Wisemen', it is far more likely that it commemorates Wish, the ghostly huntsman, who followed his shadowy pack across the moor, bringing death or ill fortune to anyone unlucky enough to see him. The spirit of the fearsome pack is still alive here. In 1982, the film makers chose this part of the moor to shoot their version of Conan Doyle's *The Hound of the Baskervilles*.

On a day of even slight mist, it is easy enough to imagine the feelings of the coffin bearers as they took their load across the West Dart to the north of this wood, and then headed to the west, leaving Longford Tor to the east and walking on towards Lydford Tor, which is still a long way from their ultimate destination. 'Ford' is simply the old name for a road, and Crossing suggests that the names of these two tors indicate that they stood on an old thoroughfare.

Certainly the track which crosses the Cowsic river at the foot of Lydford Tor [191: 592786] has long been known as Travellers' Ford. It goes past

Wistmanswood

the stone row on Conies Down, from whose height you can look north to the solitary 12-foot-high megalith of the Beardown Man on the edge of Devil's Tor, which must have served as a waymark for thousands of years. Crossing believed that the northern route of the lich path, which starts from Postbridge and the East Dart, could have joined this southerly way at some point on Conies Down, and if that is so the bearers must have crossed the swamps of Cowsic Head (now very marshy indeed) guided by that longstone on the horizon.

The southerly way does not escape the bogs, for it now goes towards the wet lands surrounding the course of the Walkham. The wicked suggestion has been made that it was here, in this remote and boggy desolation, that the bearers gave way to the temptation to lighten their load by dumping the corpse, especially if it was a pauper they were taking for burial in the parish coffin. If they did that, they disguised their trick by filling the coffin up with stones just before they reached Lydford church.

Just past White Barrow [191: 565794] the way divides as it enters the army danger area. If no red flag is flying you can follow a track that has been well used by both tinners and peat cutters going southwest to the rapidly expanding village of Peter Tavy. The true lich path is less distinct until it reaches Bagga Tor. There it joins a rough track through the bleak moor, along which quantities of peat were once conveyed on the backs of pack horses. Crossing used to meet the old men who worked on the peat diggings beneath the tor as they took their loads off the moor through Bagga Tor Gate to Wapsworthy.

This walk goes over Hill Bridge to Zoar, and

then takes the path north over Kingsett Down to the south of the army camp at Willsworthy, crosses the A386 [191: 514823] and goes northwest over Black Down to the lane which leads to Lydford.

The other branch of the lich path is known as Cut Lane. It goes from Postbridge and served the farms to the northeast of the forest. The most interesting, if not the most direct, way of reaching Postbridge from Bellever is to cross the East Dart by the clapper bridge [191: 659774] – whose central stone was removed some time in the nineteenth century – and follow the lane to Cator Common. The Walla Brook marks the forest boundary, and so in going north over Cator Common to the conifers that now cover Soussons Down and the neat little stone circle to the south of it [191: 675786], this walk runs outside the terrain of

the Lydford lich path. But the farmstead of Pizwell [191: 668785] to the west of the ford is once again in the forest, and it was the people here as well as those at Bellever who most resented the necessity of the long, sad journey to Lydford. Instead of taking their dead some 4 miles to Widecombe, they had to make for the other clapper bridge across the East Dart at Postbridge and start a weary and dangerous journey over the moor.

That bridge [191: 648789] dates from about 1200, and is one of the best preserved and certainly the most photographed of all the bridges on the moor. It was most carefully fashioned: the granite pillars are pointed to deflect the water which in winter can run to the level of the flat stones. These have not always been in their present position. In 1900 they were thrown into the water to stop the ducks swimming downstream. The path to the bridge goes past the Lydgate

Clapper bridge, Postbridge

Walk 4 The Lich Path

House Hotel, whose name at least remembers the original purpose of this track.

The main road through Postbridge, with its humped bridge, belongs to the eighteenth century. This is part of the first road to be built across the moor, and the hamlet of Postbridge grew up around it. Two enterprises were started here, encouraged by the easier means of communication. The first was the powder mill to the south of the village; the second was a starch factory, run by the brothers John and Thomas Hullett, who used potatoes grown on the moor as their raw material. The business prospered and they built the Greyhound Inn and planted the great circle of beech trees which now surrounds the car park and the National Park Information Centre.

This walk goes through much of the Hulletts' land, for although the coffins were probably carried along the drift lane on the west bank of the Dart, there is more to be seen from the slopes of Stannon Tor on the east bank of the river. So from Postbridge we start off towards Hartland House, past another of the Hulletts' impressive beech plantations.

Although the path goes along the slope of Hartland Tor [191: 642800], it is worth climbing to the top and looking across the river. From there you can see the circular patch of Broadun Ring [191: 637802], another of the old pounds of the moor, and beside it some traces of hut circles. This was once among the largest settlements on Dartmoor; traces of forty Bronze Age dwellings have been found within fourteen acres.

On the east bank there is a rather similar oblong enclosure on the slopes of Stannon Tor. It is marked on the Ordnance Survey map as The Sheepfold. Surrounded by a sizable wall, it has several smaller divisions inside which have been taken for cattle pens. No doubt the structure has been used to pen and shelter livestock, and according to Crossing it was used for that purpose by a Scotsman who was introducing one of his native breeds of sheep to the moor. This would not necessarily conflict with Theo Brown's explanation that the ruins represent the remains of the starch factory.

Just at the bend of the river there is a small

beehive hut with part of its corbelled roof still in place. Although the huts of the Bronze Age men must have looked like this, it is believed to date from a much later period and to have been used as a tinners' shelter or toolshed.

The main path from here goes north to the two stone circles of Grey Wethers, which are visited in Walk 6. The present walk goes west, following the course of the East Dart and crossing the valley through which its tributary runs. A gate in the wall along the slope of the hill to the west

[191: 636815] leads to a path above the river which flows through a little gorge. This has caused a small but powerful waterfall, and the surrounding rocks are marked by shallow saucer-shaped dips worn down by the swirling waters. This is how all the majestic rock basins on the moor have been formed.

You can either cross the river here or a little farther to the north at Sandy Hole Pass where the

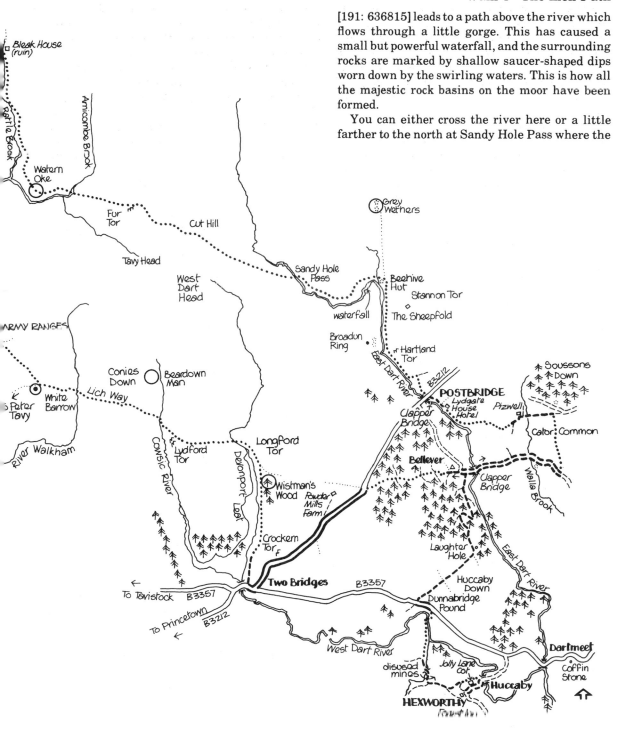

tinners used to work, and where you can see dippers flying low over the water and perching on the exposed roots of the tiny oaks that just manage to grow here. They are the last bits of obvious life that you will be seeing for some time on this walk, for from here the way to Lydford goes over a featureless waste of peat hills and swamps extending to West Dart Head. Here the fauna is composed mainly of insects, and the flora of mosses and lichens.

This area is marked by the red and white posts which outline the land used by the army. If you have miscalculated your timing and find a red flag flying here, then it means that firing could be going on, so you must retrace your steps. If it is safe to do so, make for Cut Hill [191: 598828] and the deep passage that has been cut through the peat to make travelling a little easier. Here you will find a plaque to Frank Phillpotts, brother of the writer Eden Phillpotts. Frank, who died in 1908, was responsible for the cutting of several such passages to ease the journeys of moormen and sportsmen alike.

The path to Lydford must have gone south of Fur Tor [191: 586831], although the ground around the head of the Tavey is now full of quaking bogs. Over the years the moor is getting wetter, as it takes a long time for water to drain through the granite; it is thought that the whole of the Cut Hill area could well become as barren a peat waste as Derbyshire's Kinderscout and Bleaklow. This makes some people argue in favour of extensive tree planting and welcome the activities of the Forestry Commission. They would also like to see more reservoirs, feeling that some valleys should be sacrificed to save the heights.

Whatever side you take on that discussion, you will have to make this part of the walk on the slopes of Fur Tor, and having done that it would be ridiculous not to climb it. This is the most remote of the Dartmoor tors – another of the walkers' letterboxes lies hidden among its rocks – but that is not the real purpose of the climb. Whatever Crossing said about Forest Inn, it is these rock stacks that provide the finest view over the moor. Looking west to Amicombe Brook, you can see the whole terrain that was once farmed by the Bronze Age men who lived in the large settlement of hut enclosures at Watern Oke.

Perhaps the people who once lived there, and who must have held the rocks of Fur Tor in awe, are responsible for the hold that this place still has on people's imaginations. The Aetherius Society believe it to be a natural reserve of positive energy and have made several excursions to the hill. More impressive is the story told by Ruth St Leger Gordon (*The Witchcraft and Folklore of Dartmoor*, 1965) of the sighting of a pixie here in the early 1960s. She had it from a man who had never encountered any of the little people anywhere else, but who reported that: 'The little man was seated upon one of the rocks of Fur Tor, far away from the sound or sight of humanity. This pixie was *not* dressed traditionally but wore ordinary clothes, and no word or sign passed between them. One moment the mannikin was plainly visible; the next there was nothing but the bare, grey granite.'

The western slopes of Fur Tor are dotted with rocks emerging from rough tufty grass. In the valley the Amicombe river meets the river Tavey, and at the junction of these waters is the Bronze Age settlement of Watern Oke [191: 566834]. Even in historic times this land was thought to provide the best grazing on the moor, and Crossing quotes documents referring to the pasturage here that go back six hundred years.

From Watern Oke the walk goes north along the course of the Rattle Brook, crossing the dragon line of Walk 1 at the disused ruins at the foot of Rattlebrook Hill, and continuing north towards Bleak House [191: 560865]. This remote ruin is the derelict remains of old peat workings. To the south of it, the way goes west between Arms Tor and Brat Tor, which is marked by the granite cross set up for Queen Victoria's Jubilee. It was erected by a Mr Widgery and still bears his name.

From the west of that hill, a goodish track goes through to the Dartmoor Inn on the A386. From here you will find the road to Lydford and its church, the ultimate destination of travellers along this path. The church is dedicated to the Cornish St Petroc, but I cannot say this is a conscious comment on Dartmoor's links with the Duchy.

The malign spirit that still broods over this village is of a later date. Judge Jeffreys is said to haunt the area in the guise of a large black pig, for it was here, in the formidable castle whose keep still overlooks the surrounding moor, that he held one of his Bloody Assizes. Lydford Keep is a cruel place, and still so menacing that some people cannot bring themselves to walk where offenders against the forestry laws and those who contravened the edicts of the tinners' Stannary Parliament were brought for rough justice which often ended in imprisonment, torture and death.

A happier way to end this walk is to visit the slender 100-foot waterfall which drops into the grey smooth rocks of Lydford gorge.

The gorge is on National Trust property and is a great tourist attraction, so unless you choose your time very carefully, you are unlikely to find the meditative quiet that the writer Henry Williamson enjoyed here. Yet it is always a good place, especially with the memory of such a walk as this fresh in your mind. Its narrow paths climbing through overhanging woods and crossing slabs of slippery rock make an impressive contrast to the open spaces of the vast moorland.

Wistmans Wood

Walk 5
Major Tyler's Alignments

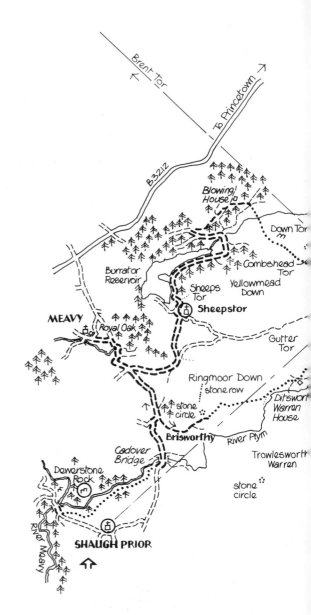

During the 1930s a certain Major F. C. Tyler (*The Geometrical Arrangement of Ancient Sites*, 1939) expanded some of the ideas put forward in Alfred Watkins's *Old Straight Track* (1922), with particular reference to his own researches in the Southwest. On Dartmoor he noted those places where three of his many alignments met, although none of these junctions is marked by any remarkable object in the landscape, and he observed how the lines he discovered often ran parallel to each other for several miles.

This walk, which starts off in the southwest and ends in the northeast corner of the moor, follows sections of three of his alignments. The first runs northwest from Shaugh Prior to the enclosure at Hunter's Tor, and the walk follows the southern part of that way as far northwest as Hartor Tors at the end of the Plym valley, after which the alignment goes through country crossed by the Abbots' Way in Walk 3. The walk follows this alignment along the northern bank of the Plym, going through one of the most fascinating archaeological sites on the whole moor.

Although the start of the alignment is at Shaugh Prior church, this walk starts from Shaugh Bridge [201: 533637] which crosses the Plym at the point where it is joined by the Meavy. From here you can scramble along the rough footpath that goes east through the woods, between the boulders that line the banks of the Plym. This path is known as the Pipe Track, because it follows the route along which a conduit was laid to carry the clay to the drying works whose ruins still stand by the bridge.

The heights of Dewerstone stand across the water. This wooded granite cliff is owned by the National Trust, which has marked out pleasant paths along its slopes. It culminates to the east in a 170-foot-high pinnacle of bare rock dotted with ivy

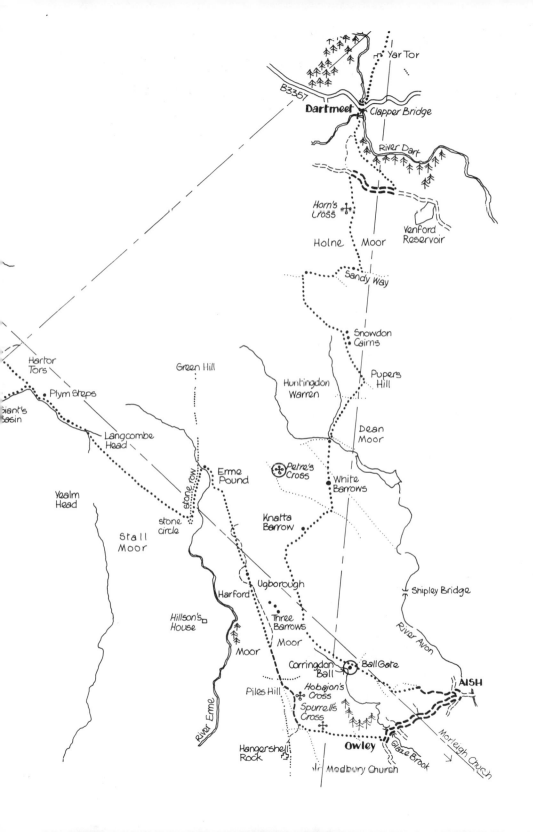

Royal oak, Meavy

and gorse bushes. This is the Devil's Rock, one of the most haunted places on the moor. The whist hounds are said to sweep through the Plym valley towards it, while their cloven-footed master leaves his footprints in the snow, sometimes accompanied by the marks of a normal five-toed foot. The rock is more permanently marked by several less supernatural inscriptions, including one to the Dartmoor poet, N. T. Carrington, who died in September 1830. In his long poem 'Dartmoor' (1826), he dared those visitors whose nerves could stand it to climb the Devil's Rock and look into 'the frightful depth beneath'. His challenge is frequently taken up by rock climbers, one of whom some twenty years ago discovered a prehistoric pot, broken in two but complete. Somehow it had found its way to a crevice in the rock. It now stands in Plymouth City Museum.

From the rock, the path by the river runs east to Cadaford or Cadover Bridge [202: 554646], passing a site of hut circles and enclosures on the opposite bank. This is the first trace of the numerous Bronze Age settlements in this valley. Although the present bridge is a modern structure, there is documentary evidence of a bridge having been here since the thirteenth century, and it is likely that there was one here long before that.

Once across the bridge, you have to decide whether to follow Tyler's alignment direct to the stone rows of Drizzlecombe in the Plym valley, or to take this opportunity to visit the village of Meavy [201: 541673] with its great hollow oak tree which is supposed to have stood here at the time of King John. The popular belief that the tree dates from the late twelfth or early thirteenth century is recorded in Loudon's *Arboretum* of 1836, which notes that it certainly predates the fifteenth-century church. The village pub, which is obviously known as the Royal Oak, has the rare distinction of being owned by the parish. Only one other pub in England has a similar management.

Just to the south of the village is the tallest of the market crosses on the moor. Marchant's Cross stands just over 8 feet and has the sign of the cross inscribed on each face. To the east of Meavy is the village of Sheepstor and the creviced granite mass of Sheeps Tor or Shittis Tor itself, surrounded by the remains of clusters of Bronze Age villages. This is supposed to be one of the main haunts of the Dartmoor pixies, and it is easy to understand how that came about if my contention that these creatures were the small early settlers in the valleys and open moorland of the neighbourhood is right. The Bronze Age inhabitants were forced to take refuge in the heights when the Saxon hordes moved in, for neither Celts nor Romans settled on the moor. This may be one reason why the Bronze Age remains are so numerous, particularly in the area of the Plym valley and on Ringmoor and Yellowmead Downs to the north of it, for the Saxons were a superstitious race, and were afraid of the settlements of the people they conquered.

There is an ancient local tradition that promises such great wealth to whoever finds the treasure of Ringmoor Down that he may thereafter plough with a golden ploughshare and yoke his oxen with golden cross-sticks. Perhaps that hope caused the searching and scratching that revealed the real treasure of the down, the tin discovered in Brisworthy just to the north of Cadover Bridge. That discovery was made in 1168 and the find caused something of a gold rush to the area. Prospectors rushed to the place and, within a decade, Dartmoor was established as the richest source of tin in Europe.

For most visitors today, the treasure of these downs lies in the landscape itself with its structures of sacred standing stones. Yellowmead Down has one of the most elaborate cairns on the moor. It is enclosed within four retaining circles which have been recently restored, and there is clear evidence that at least one stone row approached it from the west. To the north, Burrator Reservoir has made the countryside alpine with conifers and water. Yet Dartmoor asserts its own character still: the paths through the trees are dotted with traces of the tinners' workings, drainage leats and blowing houses. For once the twentieth-century needs for wood and water blend well with those of earlier ages, and it is a pleasure to walk here.

The eastern edge of the forest is crossed by another of Tyler's alignments. It runs from Brent

Tor on the northwestern edge of the moor to Moreleigh church which lies just outside it to the southeast. The line crosses Down Tor [202: 580694] and Combshead Tor [202: 588689], and goes just to the west of the stone circle which stands between them and which is approached by an irregular stone row made up of 160 stones. If we go southeast from here, past a disused tin mine and across the track which runs north to Nun's Cross Farm (see page 33), we come to the point where this second alignment crosses the one from Shaugh Prior as it passes through Drizzlecombe.

Before going over Plym Steps [202: 604672] and following this second line southeast to Corringdon Ball burial chamber [202: 669614], it is essential to give some time to Drizzlecombe itself. If you have come this way from Meavy or Sheepstor, you will reach the valley by the hut circles of Gutter Tor; from Cadover Bridge you approach it by the stone circle to the south of Ringmoor Down. Either way you come to the entrance to the valley of the stone rows by way of Ditsworthy Warren House [202: 585663], a long-uninhabited farm now owned by the National Park, and boasting a brilliant green pasture where animals have grazed for centuries.

The path behind the farm runs down to the wide, shallow valley of the Plym, with Hartor Tors on the eastern skyline. Here are three great standing stones, the tallest of which is 14 feet. Each monolith stands at the head of a stone row which ends in a cairn. In the middle of this complex there is a large barrow, and further cairns and cists lie to the east. The most important of these is the Giant's Basin [202: 593670]. It gets its name from the large crater in the top, the scar of some early excavation. The whole thing extends over a hundred acres, and at one time held a granite chamber, a 'pixie cave', capable of serving as a burial chamber for several bodies.

The area on the south side of the Plym is almost as rich in Bronze Age remains as the downs around Sheepstor to the north. To the west is the stone circle, with its accompanying stone row, by Trowlesworthy Warren [202: 578640], a ceremonial site which served the people living in the six nearby enclosures, the remaining walls of which are still 9 feet thick in places. The warren itself dates from the thirteenth century when rabbits vied with tin as the main resource of the moor.

Going south from the Plym valley, the walk follows the second of Tyler's alignments as it goes southeast towards the Bronze Age settlements of Stall Moor. The alignment runs directly to the stone circle [202: 635644] to the north of that land, but in order to have a fairly dry walk, it is best to approach it obliquely, keeping on a course between Langcombe and Yealm Heads.

The stone circle is at the southern tip of the longest stone row on Dartmoor, and probably in the world. It extends for over 2 miles to the north, ending at the cairn on the top of Green Hill, its stones varying a little in size but none exceeding 5½ feet. It is a single line curving slightly to the east to avoid climbing Stinger's Hill and in order to make an easier crossing of the Erme. The stones are clearly visible from some distance as they run out over the bare ground. Like most standing stones, they resemble sheep to me, but Baring-Gould was more original. He saw this row as 'a procession of cricketers in flannels stalking over the moor'. This walk follows the row north as far as the river crossing by Erme Pound [202: 641653], and from there goes south through a thick cluster of enclosures and hut circles above the river to join the wide track that runs south between Harford and Ugborough Moors.

At this point, if the weather is clear, it is worth scrambling right up to the height of Three Barrows [202: 653626], from where you can look back across the River Erme to the southern part of Stall Moor, with its remnants of hut circles and tinners' dwellings. By a cairn on the hillside is the ruin of Hillson's House [202: 638624]. Hillson was a watchmaker who, in this remote place, made a living with his eight-day clocks. The story goes that in choosing to live here, and in building a house made of stones from the cairns, he was returning to his origins, for he was a true son of the hill, having been found there as an infant waif and brought up by some good people who gave him his name.

The path goes over Piles Hill to Hobajons Cross [202: 655605], which is not a cross at all but a rough boundary mark. The track, locally known as Blackwood Path because it was once mainly used for the carriage of peat, extends as far south as Bittaford. On its way it crosses another stone row on the ridge above Hangershell Rock.

Those who believe that the stone rows marked out some sort of ceremonial racecourse will find backing for their theories here. Up to 1870, moorland horse races were held in this place, the course being marked out by stones to the east of the rock. It could be that the people who raced their horses here were carrying on a tradition started by Bronze Age people, who, like the Magyars and Finns, prized horses swift enough to win the ceremonial races, the winners of which took the greater share of the dead man's goods. Documents left by Anglo-Saxon travellers tell us that in those foreign lands the dead man's goods were piled up by the burial cairn at the end of the ceremonial racecourse, and the young men contesting for the inheritance were allocated their share in proportion to the order in which they reached the winning post.

North of the rock a path goes east to Spurrell's Cross [202: 665599], the only example of a Dartmoor cross with stretched limbs. Here the walk joins the third of Tyler's alignments. This one runs from Modbury church to the south of the moor to a point to the northwest of Spinsters' Rock, near Drewsteignton, in the north. In the seventeenth century the path that runs by Spurrell's Cross was a road linking Harford to the west with South Brent to the east. We follow it down to Owley, then take the lane across the Glaze Brook to Aish, climbing back onto the moor by the track leading to Ball Gate [202: 670614] and the Neolithic burial chamber of Corringdon Ball [202: 669614], a tomb dating from the fourth millenium BC, the only certain Neolithic barrow on Dartmoor.

From here a rough path goes below the Three Barrows on Ugborough Moor towards Knatta Barrow [202: 659643]. When the path meets the one that joins Petre's Cross to Shipley Bridge, the way goes straight ahead over White Barrows [202: 665652], crosses the Abbots' Way to the southwest of Dean Moor, and continues north through the abandoned tin working to the east of Huntingdon Warren. Both the alignment and the course of this walk go over Pupers Hill and Snowdon [202: 669684] to Sandy Way, the old track leading from the village of Holne, birthplace of Charles Kingsley, to the grazing grounds of the high moor which extends as far west as Childe's Tomb (see page 33). Leaving that old track, Major Tyler's alignment goes due north towards Dartmeet, a place ironically written off as a 'sacrifice area' by the National Park Authority, who have given it up entirely to tourist amenities.

They are soon shaken off. The way north goes along the western slopes of Yar Tor [191: 675743], past another stone row standing above the Walla Brook, a water that was crossed by a clapper bridge until the floods of 4 August 1826 destroyed it. A path goes over Cator Common to Soussons Down, and from there to Warren House Inn the way coincides with the walk from Widecombe (see page 26).

After this path leaves the forty-year-old forest, it goes through disused mine workings to Bennett's Cross [191: 684816] to the east of the B3212. Theo Brown claims that the name Bennett comes from *benet*, a clerk in minor orders whose function was to act as an exorcist. She makes that the reason for believing that the cross is pre-Reformation, and had been there for a long time when it was mentioned as a boundary mark in a document of 1702. The WB inscribed on the stone stands for 'Warren Bounds', another indication of the commercial importance of rabbits in the economy of the moor.

From the inn, a path goes over Chagford Common towards Metherall [191: 674839], and the lane that goes northeast from there to Chagford is part of an old road, shown on a fifteenth-century map of the moor, leading from that Stannary town to Tavistock. As the moor around Chagford forms the basis of the last walk in this section, which traces the concentric circles that Richard Long drew around Fernworthy, this can be an opportunity to visit Chagford itself [191: 702877].

This Stannary town is now one of the main centres of the living folk tradition of Dartmoor, fostering several moormen who perpetuate the old songs and dances. Perhaps its strong links with

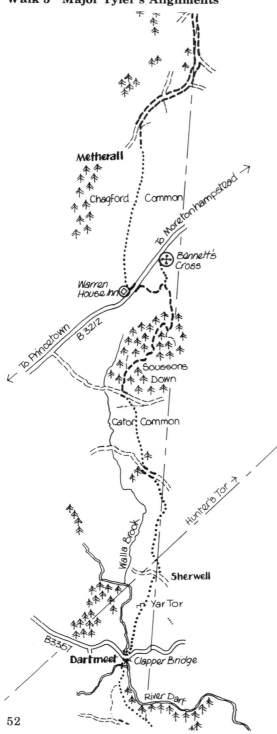

Metherall

Chagford   Common

To Moretonhampstead →

Bennett's Cross

Warren House Inn

← To Princetown

B 3212

Soussons Down

Cator Common

Hunter's Tor →

Walla Brook

Sherwell

Yar Tor

B 3357

Dartmeet   Clapper Bridge

River Dart

the past were forged during the nineteenth century, for from 1799 to 1925 the town had only three schoolmasters, which must have given the people a feeling of continuity. The school these good men taught in is now used as the British Legion Hall. It stands next to the Three Crowns Hotel, a building that dates from the thirteenth century and which retains far more of its original fabric than the church, originally dedicated to St Michael the Archangel on 30 July 1261, but mostly rebuilt in the fifteenth century. Here there is a chapel dedicated to St Katherine, the patron saint of tinners.

Tyler's alignment goes through the crossroads to the northwest of the town by Way Down [191: 693893]. Here this walk parts company with it for good, for while the alignment heads due north, leaving Spinsters' Rock to the east, we take the lane across the A382 to that Neolithic monument. There is nothing left of the barrow which once stood here; what we have is a quoit, consisting of three uprights and a capstone, put into their present position after the original structure collapsed in the mid-nineteenth century. But the quoit, standing in a small field opposite a farm flanked by two lanes, has attracted its own legend. They say that the burial chamber was built early one morning by three spinsters.

To take yourself from the Neolithic to the Edwardian age, go to Edward Lutyen's outrageous oddity of Castle Drogo [191: 720903] on the heights overlooking Teign Gorge. It is a place where Tyler himself would surely have felt at home, for it is redolent of the era before the social upheavals of the 1940s. Designed for the Mr Drew who founded Home and Colonial Grocers, it has all the romance, and few of the discomforts (if you discount the servants' quarters underground), of a medieval fortress. The building is now owned by the National Trust and open to visitors.

From there you can walk along the banks of the Teign to Fingle Bridge [191: 744901], and immediately you are back in prehistory. To the east are the visible but inaccessible earthworks of Prestonbury Castle, and across the bridge, to the southwest of the path climbing through Hannicombe Wood, is Cranbrook Castle, whose fortifications stand on the height of Up-

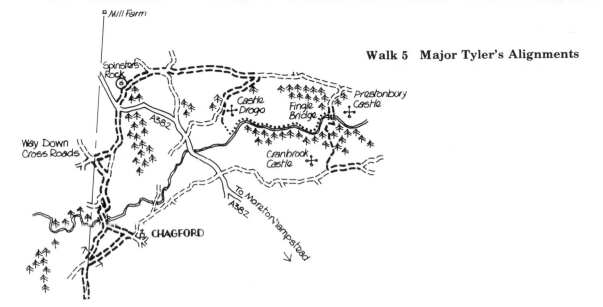

pacott Down. Both forts belong to the Iron Age.

This is the rich agricultural edge of the moor, and it probably was so when cattle were herded into these hilltop settlements which overlook the steep banks of the Teign Gorge, still clothed in woods that the Celts would find familiar. Now, looking back over the moor on a mist-free day, you can see as they did the heights of Cosdon to the north and the two granite stacks of Hey Tor. Only the fields of Gidleigh and Throwleigh, where the next walk ends, mark the changes of the centuries. When Prestonbury and Cranbrook were inhabited, those fields were full of people whose settlements we are still able to trace.

view from Cranbrook Castle

Walk 6
Richard Long's Circles

Richard Long has inscribed at least two patterns on Dartmoor. In one he used the whole extent of the moor, and claimed to visit a hundred tors in a hundred hours. In the other, which forms the basis of this walk, he made an even more curious connection between space and time. He took four concentric circles to the west of Fernworthy and made the circumference of each of them correspond to an hour's walk. This walk ignores the small central circle and picks up his strange pattern at the equally mysterious nineteenth-century reconstructions of the twin stone circles of Grey Wethers [191: 638822], an operation for which, almost needless to say, the Reverend Sabine Baring-Gould was largely responsible.

The walk starts along the lane from Metherall [191: 674839] on the south bank of the reservoir created in 1934. Beneath its waters lies the old settlement of Fernworthy, where the Lightfoots farmed from the late seventeenth century. The lane reaches the forest by an old boundary stone. The conifers here, which have destroyed the countryside that support them almost as thoroughly as the reservoir has obliterated the farms, have many Bronze Age relics hidden among the trees. At least the Forestry Commission has taken the trouble to preserve them, a piece of conservation which might not automatically have taken place if the land had been sold to a private concern.

To the south of the path, on the slopes of Assycombe Hill, a double stone row climbs 60 feet in the space of 40 yards, and the path running northwest from there passes the sites of a stone circle and another stone row, as well as several hut enclosures. All these monuments were no doubt familiar to the owner of the copper knife which was discovered together with a cloak button and a long-necked beaker, in the cistvaen, or single stone burial place, here. The pines would astonish

him, for he moved among the small oak trees which are believed to have grown at this altitude during the warm climate of the Bronze Age.

The path comes out of the forest onto the long ridge that runs south towards Postbridge. This walk follows it south to the stones of the Grey Wethers. Before reconstruction, the northerly one had only nine standing stones, while the one to the south had seven. Their original numbers must have been considerable, for these are large circles, both having diameters of over 100 feet, and they must once have formed the chief temple in an area encrusted with the remains of Bronze Age settlers. Their huts sheltered beneath Sittaford Tor, which is crowned with a logan stone to which magical powers were probably ascribed.

From that stone, the walk goes west across Richard Long's circles to the ruined stone hut of Statts House [191: 623825], where there is another of the moor's letterboxes. On the slopes of Winney's Down you can walk along another path through the peat, originally cut in the early years of this century for the benefit of hunters and cattle men, at the instigation of Frank Phillpotts.

From here, provided no red flags are flying (for you are on army ground), the walk goes beyond Long's circles to the East Dart, follows the river north for a mile or so, and then climbs eastwards over the hill to the Teign valley. If you come this way in high summer, you will make the walk through a mass of bog asphodel. At the crossing of the infant Teign, below Quintin's Man [191: 622838], there is yet another letterbox.

This oddly named hill is topped by two army huts and a cairn. Here we walk away from Richard Long's circles and follow the way the peat cutters went towards Batworthy [191: 662865]. The way goes through the Varracombe valley towards Teignhead Farm [191: 635844] over ground which

hut circle, Fernworthy Reservoir

has suffered severe subsidence on account of intensive peat cutting. The farm is now deserted for no one of recent years has apparently felt able to cope with the loneliness of this remote site. It was once used as a centre for summer grazing by the Endicott family, which provided the last reeve of Dartmoor, and whose descendant, Robert Harris, an architect, now runs a shop devoted to folklore interests in the village of Hatherleigh to the north of Okehampton.

The old farm road goes down to a crossing of the Teign, and the walk goes north of Fernworthy

Stone Row
Shovel down

56

Forest towards the 10-foot-high Longstone [191: 660856] on Shovel Down, one of a dramatic concentration of monuments. They include two double stone rows running north to south; a possible stone circle to the northwest of these; and a circle made of four stone rings surrounding a cairn to the south. There is also a single stone row which runs from the Longstone itself and traces of another double row leading to a 4-foot-high standing stone. To the southeast of that there is a stone cist.

To the east the rock of Kestor [191: 665864] stands out from the bare slope of the moor. Its granite is worn into rock basins which may have been used as part of the rituals practised by the Bronze and Iron Age people who farmed this region. They left traces of their field systems on the moor, and their enclosures and dwelling places are

still marked out by the granite slabs on the southern slopes.

The most spectacular of these enclosures is the Round Pound [191: 665874]. It stands to the north of the lane from Teigncombe and is made up of two concentric circles. The inner one is the remains of a large dwelling, while the space between it and the outer circle is divided into wedge-shaped sections which are presumably once used as animal pens and outbuildings. Their walls still provide sheep with shelter from the winds.

The lane across the moor leads west towards Batworthy, a flourishing farm once owned by a Mr F. N. Budd, who in the last years of the nineteenth century collected over 6000 specimens of flint implements – arrow heads, knives and scrapers – from his land. Obviously some sort of Stone Age factory was in operation here for there were flakes and nodules among the worked flints. Many of the latter were composed of the brown chert which is found on the beach at Sidmouth, and so Mr Budd reasonably supposed that there was some sort of a trade route from this part of the moor going east across the Exe.

From Batworthy, make for the wide clapper bridge [191: 655873] that goes across the Teign. That takes you onto Gidleigh Common, and the twenty-three standing stones of Scorhill Circle, which is aligned to the stone row of Shovel Down, although in summer a windbreak of beeches makes it impossible to appreciate that pattern. By the time that circle was erected, the land of Gidleigh Common had been settled for thousands of years. From the Mesolithic period, the people who used the flints discovered by Mr Budd were hunter–gatherers around this edge of the moor. When they started fires to drive their prey from the trees, they began the clearance of the primeval forests, thus enabling the Bronze Age families to settle here in such numbers, and later making it possible for the Celts to farm this land.

A gate to the east of Scorhill Circle takes us off the moor and onto the lanes of Gidleigh. These run through land which the Saxons occupied and cultivated. Post holes discovered here beneath early medieval stone long houses prove that the early Saxon inhabitants kept to their usual custom and

built their dwellings of wattle and turf, despite the plentiful availability of building stone. We know from much Anglo-Saxon verse that these people had a superstitious dread of ruined places, and possibly this fear prevented them from using the stone that fashioned the houses of the people they conquered. Yet Gidleigh gets its name from a royal Saxon, whose son was to be conquered by an even more powerful foe, for it was once the property of Gydda or Gythia, mother of King Harold.

After the death of her son, she is supposed to have taken refuge farther to the east on the limestone rock of Steep Holm in the Bristol Channel.

Our walks now take us westwards into Cornwall, but Chagford, about three miles along the lanes from Kestor, is a good place to take leave of Dartmoor. As I have said, a little while spent in the bar of the Three Crowns will convince you that anything that happens on Dartmoor soon becomes Chagford's business.

Part Two Bodmin

Focal Points

Brown Willy 201: 158800
Bury Castle 200: 135696
Castle-an-Dinas 200: 945625
Castle Dore 200: 104548
Cheesewring 201: 253724
Crowpound 201: 175678
Dozmary Pool 201: 195745
Fernacre Circle 200: 145799
Fourhole Cross 201: 172750
Golant 200: 121552
Hurlers 201: 256714
King Arthur's Bed 201: 242757
King Arthur's Hall 200: 129777
Leaze Circle 200: 137774
Longstone 200: 061734
Long Tom 201: 255705
Middlemoor Cross 200: 125794
Nine Maidens 200: 935675
Old Cardinham Castle 200: 126680
Restormel Castle 200: 105614
Rough Tor 200: 145808
St Clether's Well 201: 204848
St Endellion 200: 996786
St Enedoc 200: 932773
St Neot's Well 201: 182680
Slaughterbridge 200: 109855
Stannon Circle 200: 125798
Stripple Stones 200: 144753
Tintagel Castle 200: 051889
Trethevy Quoit 201: 258688
Tristan Stone 200: 109525

Part Two Bodmin

. . . another to Cornwall, where granite resists
the sea and our type of thinking ends.

W. H. Auden, 'Address for a Prize Day', from
The Orators, 1932

I have heard it said that the wave-battered, narrow peninsula of Cornwall produces vibrations
that really do alter the rhythm of people's emo-
tional climate. It is as though moods were
deepened with the shock of the waves on slate and
granite and were chained to the relentless sawing
of the tides. Whether that is fanciful or not, no one
will dispute that a crossing of the Tamar is as
significant a venture as a crossing of the Channel.
Cornwall is not England; nor is it completely
homogeneous in itself, as the walks over two of its
four granite moors will prove.

From Dartmoor it was possible to see the
heights of Bodmin, the first of the moors, but to get
the clearest idea of the way ahead, the best thing
to do after crossing that dividing river, is to climb
up Kit Hill [201: 375714]. You can reach it by
footpath from Callington, or by driving from
Monkscross and turning up the lane by the
Methodist chapel; a 10p toll road will take you to
the top. Despite the tumuli on the south side of the
hill and the earthwork on its summit, this is not a
beautiful place. The road, the old quarry workings, the concrete shed and the great ugly monu-
mental tower have destroyed whatever charm or
symmetry it may once have had. But it does provide the most extensive view of the countryside
around. Three charts by the monument map out
the viewpoints.

The most remarkable features are the summits
of Rough Tor and Brown Willy, Cornwall's highest
hills, and the chimneys of the various mine workings which cover the country. From Kit Hill the
nearest mines are the Holmbush group to the
north of Callington, which were in operation in
the early seventeenth century. Another working
between here and Bodmin Moor is near New-
bridge on the banks of the river Lynher, but the
ones we shall encounter on the walks across the

Hut circle
Rough Tor

moor are at the head of that river, by Fivelanes
near Altarnun, where both tin and copper were
worked; those around Trewortha and Twelve
Men's Moor, which were active in the sixteenth
century; and the tall brick chimneys around the
stone circles of The Hurlers on Craddock Moor.

Like that of the rest of Cornwall, the rich geol-
ogy of Bodmin has been exploited for centuries.
The visitor who is looking for traces of the settlements and ritual sites of Bronze Age farmers, or
for the marks of Arthurian legends, will find them
intermingled with industrial relics and with
present-day workings whose marks on the land-

scape vary from the dark grey of the 500-foot-deep slate quarry at Delabole to the shimmering white and metallic blue of the china clay works on Stannon Down, and the white mountains of clay around St Austell to the southwest of the moor.

Yet despite all this industry, Bodmin Moor itself, which extends about 10 miles in each direction, can be a wild and lonely place, much more like Dartmoor than Exmoor. Its own remote and inscrutable character is epitomized for many visitors by the still waters of Dozmary Pool with its Arthurian legend of Excalibur and the traces of Mesolithic inhabitants who left their beautifully worked flint tools around its shores. For me, the most memorable part of Bodmin is the valley between Rough Tor and Brown Willy, where the Bronze Age men farmed and met to worship their gods and perpetuate the glory of their ancestors at the stone circles they erected.

The paths we shall take pass close to the skyline burials of the chiefs of these people. Their funeral fires must have been visible for miles around; and as they died down, the fresh barrows, clear of the turf and bracken that we see now, and sometimes made deliberately more conspicuous by the use of imported, contrasting earth, would have been a constant reminder to passing travellers of the great leaders who once herded cattle and cultivated their crops on this land. There are Iron Age forts and settlements, some of which make use of the natural strongholds, such as that formed by the rocky outcrop of the Cheesewring. They were used by the Celts who came to Bodmin during the first century BC, and whose language was to become the native speech of Cornwall, linked to Welsh and Breton.

It is a British Celt, of the Dark Ages, whose legend haunts this moor. I believe that Arthur was not one individual but a glorified amalgam of all those Romano-British chieftains who set out to defend the newly Christianized people when the legions left them to the mercy of the pagan Saxons. It is partly thanks to Tennyson that this part of Cornwall has become so rich in Arthurian lore, but the tradition goes farther back, and Tintagel has become as vital as Glastonbury in its associations with the great king, his wizard and his knights. On the moor itself many natural features and one almost inexplicable earthworks are connected with his name.

More solid, if more anonymous, are the ruins of the medieval farmhouses of the moor, and the stone crosses which guide today's walkers as they have guided travellers for centuries along the ridges and valleys. It is a relief to find them, for the mists can come down here as rapidly as they do on Dartmoor, and the land is quite as wet and boggy. Although the ground here will never tremble beneath your boots in quite such an alarming way as it does on the Dartmoor heights, the bogs which began to form around 900 BC are every bit as deep and dangerous.

Many of the crosses now stand by the roadsides, and so are not necessarily encountered in the walks across the moor. One such is the Longstone near the village of St Mabyn, whose story is connected with a smith who lived at the time of King Arthur. This smith waged a continuous war with the Devil and, in the account related by M. A. Courtney (*Cornish Feasts and Folklore*, 1890), he finally challenged him to a reaping contest, which he won by the dodge of scattering harrow tines all over the Devil's acre. When the Devil saw that he was losing, he flung his whetstone at the smith and flew off. So holy was the devious smith that the Devil's stone which martyred him became a cross.

Although no stones are likely to be flung, it is important for the walker to remember that Bodmin is not a National Park. Apart from the walk up the north side of Rough Tor, which has been given to the public as part of a war memorial, the moor is privately owned farmland, interspersed with commons, whose grazing rights are only extended to the people who live around them. So the walker makes his way by courtesy of the landowners, and must respect the privilege, leave when asked to do so, and never trespass on any intake, those parts of the moor which have been fenced off for pastoral or arable farming.

On the open moorland there are herds of ponies, flocks of sheep, and a few Highland cattle and belted Galloways, such as we found on Dartmoor. As for wild life – the most significant creature is

The Cheesewring

missing. They say that the last pair of Cornish choughs died out in Rocky Valley near Tintagel. So there is no hope of seeing that emblem of the county, the elegant crow with the red beak and long red legs into which, some say, Arthur was changed after his death. The other story is that the chough is Merlin in disguise, keeping an eye open to judge the time when Arthur should be re-awakened. The birds you will see in some numbers, however, are the buzzards and kestrels, and the magpies, which seem even larger here than elsewhere. They increase and flourish now that they are no longer shot for food.

The walks I have described across this moor follow five routes. The first goes along another section of the dragon path to Land's End. This path passes through The Hurlers, by the village of Min-

ions on the south side of the moor. The second walk follows the routes that the Celtic saints and prehistoric traders took from the mouth of the Camel in the north to the Fowey estuary in the south. The part that river played in the life and trade of the moor is marked by the fact that the whole area was known as Fowey Moor (not Bodmin Moor) up to the late Middle Ages. The third walk is in the north; it leaves the moor to explore the area between Tintagel and Padstow where the saints set up their first settlements on Cornish soil. The fourth starts from the town of Bodmin itself and follows the trader's routes to the east; and the last walk traces the lines, discerned by a Victorian writer, A. R. Lewis (*Journal of the Royal Institute of Cornwall*, 1898), which links the stone circles of the northern part of the moor.

Walk 7
The Dragon Path to Land's End

The eastern side of Bodmin Moor is bounded by the river Lynher, and it is at Rilla Mill [201: 295732], where the present road bridge crosses the river, that the dragon path to Land's End enters Bodmin Moor. From Rilla Mill it runs to Upton Cross. Both of these villages have suffered badly from bungaloid development, so that it is now almost impossible to appreciate their original individual character. They owe their existence to the nineteenth-century copper mines, whose gaunt ruined engine houses add to the extraordinary character of this part of the moor.

Just before the lane reaches Minions (a couple of miles from Upton Cross), a sign on the right points to the Cheesewring, which stands 1 mile to the north. It is well worth taking that path and making the brief circular walk that comes round to the three stone circles of The Hurlers [201: 256714] behind Minions village. The track to the Cheesewring is the more western of two parallel roads to the old mines and quarries. It crosses the invisible dragon line and passes a large cairn of stones and turf. This is the Rillaton Barrow [201: 260719]. On its eastern side is a stone cist from which the fully extended skeleton of a man was dug up in 1818. His position was unusual, for in Bronze Age burials such as this the bodies were almost invariably trussed into a foetal position. It was obviously some great man who was given this unusual treatment, for rare treasures were placed with him in the grave: a dagger of the type associated with the rich Wessex culture to the east, blue faience beads made of carefully combined glass and clay and possibly imported from Egypt or Mycenae, and an elaborate gold cup. This treasure is now in the British Museum, but for a long time

The Hurlers

the gold cup was missing. The excavator who discovered it some years after the exhumation of the body gave it to Queen Victoria as treasure trove, after which the records of its whereabouts became confused. No one knew where it was until the archaeologist, Christopher Hawkes, finally concluded his persistent search by trying Buckingham Palace. It was discovered there, being used as an ashtray by George V.

The gold cup was also a source of folklore and tradition. At the end of the nineteenth century, Baring-Gould mentioned the local belief that a prophet who once dwelt near the Cheesewring owned a cup of gold that could never be drained. It was his custom to offer it to passing hunters to quench their thirst. One day one of them determined to drain the cup dry and drank until he could hold no more. The cup still was not empty. Furious at his failure, he threw the contents in the prophet's face and tried to make off with the treasure. But he did not get very far, both he and his horse were killed falling over the edge of the rocks.

Beyond Rillaton Barrow is the rocky outcrop of Stowe's Pound, an Iron Age hill fort whose defences were built out of the natural crags. The Cheesewring [201: 253724] balances on the southern side above a quarry which has been cut in the slope of the hill beneath. The top stone of this gravity-defying pile of rocks is said to turn round three times when it hears the cock crow; and the pile gets its name from its partial resemblance to a cider-making press, for the apple pulp in that process is called 'cheese'.

Just beside it, also on the edge of the quarry, there is a stone carved with the name of D. Gumb and the date 1735. It commemorates an eccentric stone cutter, philosopher and mathematician from Linkinhorne on the eastern side of the moor who took his wife and family to the remote house which he built on the slope of the hill which has now been destroyed by the quarry. There he meditated on the figures from Euclid which he cut into the rock roof of his dwelling. These figures were seen by a John Harris of Liskeard who was taken to visit the sage as a child, and who later recorded the occasion; but any visitor to Linkinhorne churchyard can judge of Gumb's skill as a stone mason.

The northeastern defences of the enclosure of Stowe's Pound look towards Dartmoor, those to the south face the stone rings of The Hurlers. The direct way from the Cheesewring to those circles runs due south. About half a mile to the west of that path there is an extensive old quarry, which in disuse has become a place of fantasy, with random steep towers and deep clear pools which look as though they had been landscaped by a giant.

The dragon line runs through The Hurlers. These stones are a mystery. Apart from the old legend that they are the petrified bodies of men punished for playing the game of hurling on the Sabbath, very little has been put forward to explain these carefully sited circles, once linked to each other by a paved causeway. We only know that a large area of the northern circle was paved with a granite slab; that there was a single stone in the centre of the middle one; and that the original circle builders found it important to make sure that all the stones projected to the same height

above the ground, an effect they achieved by sinking them in holes of different depths. We cannot know why these circles were so elaborately designed; they retain their mystery. It was once thought that it was not even possible to count the stones which define them. A seventeenth-century visitor to the site explained how that problem at least was resolved. 'They are easily numbered,' he wrote, 'but the people had a story that they never were till a man took many penny loafes and laying one on each hurler did comput by the remainder what number they were.' The current count is thirty-nine altogether, and it is estimated that each circle was initially made up of between twenty-five and thirty-five stones.

To the west of the circles there are two outriders which frame the Cheesewring, and a little farther off is a memorial stone of 1846, a sad instance of unwitting Victorian vandalism, which set an unhappy precedent for the erection of memorials throughout the moors.

From The Hurlers, the dragon path continues southwest over Craddock Moor past the farms of Chy [201: 254714] and Trewalla [201: 245711], flanked by a cairn and a tumulus. It then goes across the moorland lying below the southern part of the Siblyback Reservoir.

If it is a clear day, and not too wet, it is possible to follow this course of the line over the marshes to the cross that stands just to the south of Crylla Farm [201: 239705]. From there the walk goes by farm tracks around the reservoir in an anticlockwise direction to Trekeivesteps [201: 228700] where it joins the dragon path again.

Another route goes along the lane that runs due south over Common Moor to King Doniert's Stone [201: 235688], a point which can also be reached by the unfenced road from Minions, which offers pleasant walks along its moorland verges. About half a mile from that village is Long Tom [201: 255705], a longstone standing 9 feet high, and possibly a distant outrider to The Hurlers.

Trethevy Quoit
Bodmin

Since the time that it served that function, it has been carved with a Christian cross, and was no doubt a waymark to medieval travellers, who may have moved it to its present position.

From here lanes run by the village of Darite to Trethevy Quoit [201: 258688], which was known up to the nineteenth century as the Giant's House. It is in fact the remains of a chamber tomb which once stood within a Neolithic long barrow of the early fourth millennium BC. John Norden, whose *Description of Cornwall* was written four hundred years ago, described it as 'a little house raised of mightie stones standing on a little hill within a fielde.' The hill, which was the remains of the earth mound of the barrow, has now disappeared. From the quoit a footpath goes to the village of St Cleer, whose well was once celebrated as a 'boussening' or ducking well for the cure of mad people.

This hilltop village on the edge of the moor quadrupled its size in the mid-nineteenth century when the copper mines of Craddock Moor and Caradon Hill brought unlimited work to the area. That seeming prosperity was not entirely an unmixed blessing. A miner was reckoned to have a life expectancy of seventeen years from the day he first entered the pits as a lad of fifteen or so, and wages were never high enough to recompense the families in any way for the early death of the breadwinner. Yet a certain gloss of Victorian wellbeing hung over the public buildings in the village, as you can see from the sixteenth-century chapel which stands over the well itself, and which was carefully restored in the middle of the last century. It stands by the roadside, surrounded by the new houses that have sprung up here since the 1960s. It is protected by a low stone wall and consists of a steeply roofed stone canopy supported on six arches.

From the village the lane runs northwest to King Doniert's Stone. There are in fact two stones in the enclosure in which it stands. The king's stone is the one nearest to the road, and the inscription on it can still be plainly read: *'Doniert rogavit pro anima'* (Doniert has asked [prayers] for his soul). Also known as Dungarth, he was the last of the Cornish kings, and met his death by drowning in Fowey river in 878.

Almost directly opposite this stone is a footpath going across the moor to the lane leading to Trekeivesteps. From there it is possible to walk along the dragon line to the hill fort [201: 198689] among the old mine workings of Berry Down, but it is not a route to be attempted in poor weather for it runs across difficult open country, crossing the two farm roads that traverse Draynes Common. A footpath from the road to the southwest of the common goes to Berry Down Fort, which, like Stowe's Pound, makes use of the natural rock as part of its defences. Within the compound are a number of hut circles, and the whole encampment lies on the slope of the hill protected from the prevailing northwest wind.

The dragon path goes downhill to the lane, and there this walk temporarily parts from it and makes for the village of St Neot, rejoining it at St Neot's Well [201: 182680]. This stands on the bank of the river, marked on the OS maps as St Neot river, but locally known by its more pleasing thirteenth-century name of Loveny.

The well lies beyond the fifteenth-century church in the village, in whose churchyard there is a heavily ornamented shaft of a Saxon cross, all that remains of a much earlier building. Inside the church there is stained glass which can rival the famous windows of Fairford in the Cotswolds. It dates mainly from the late fifteenth and early sixteenth centuries, and its restoration by John Hedgeland in the 1820s shows more sensitivity than most nineteenth-century church work.

Among the panels illustrating the Creation, at the east end of the south aisle, there is one that shows a story almost peculiar to Cornwall. It concerns the death of Adam. According to medieval legend, first written down in the fourteenth century by the canons of the Cornish collegiate house of Glasney, Seth undertook a journey to the gates of Paradise to beg the oil of mercy for his father. The cherubim told him to take three pips from the apple his father ate and, as soon as the old man died, to put them between his teeth and tongue. Three trees grew from these seeds, as you can see in the window, and in one of them is the Christ Child holding the precious oil.

More pertinent to the dragon line, however, is

the window that shows the life of St George and his restoration by the Virgin Mary after his fight with the serpent. There are no St Michael churches on this particular stretch of the dragon line, but the perennial struggle is recalled in this form.

It is, however, St Neot's Well, and not the church, that stands on the alignment. They say that this well provided the saint with a daily supply of fish, in thanksgiving for which he stood up to his neck in its waters reciting the whole of the Psalter. There is a little Victorian building round it now, replacing an earlier stone arch. The curative powers of this water were felt to be so strong that delicate children were brought long distances to bathe in it on the first three mornings of May.

The next point on the dragon path is Crowpound [201: 175678], a rectangular earthwork which is said to get its name from the story that St Neot impounded the crows there, so that the farmers would have no excuse for not attending church. Unfortunately for the veracity of that good story, *crow* probably does not refer to the bird at all, but to the Cornish word for a cross. The origins of the earthwork itself are uncertain. Some scholars date it in the Bronze Age, others believe it was a medieval cattle pound.

From that place the walk goes west to Pantersbridge, which gets its name from the early fifteenth-century bridge that stands beside the modern road. This is a good place to end the walk, although it is possible to rejoin the dragon line at Trevorder and follow it through to the edge of the moor, where it crosses the trunk road.

Walk 8
Saints and Tinners

Tintagel

Three themes come together in this walk across the moor from Tintagel to Fowey: the travels of the Celtic saints across the peninsula on their way from Ireland and Wales to Brittany; the tinners who were taking their wares to the southern ports; and many of the legends of King Arthur. To incorporate the latter I have cheated a little, for the more direct route for the travelling saints ran from the mouth of the Camel, at Padstow, to the west of this walk, so some of the roads they followed are described in Walk 9.

Wherever they started from, as they journeyed south the saints must often have been in company with the tinners, who may even then have shared the belief, common to their Elizabethan descendants, that the tin streams were washed down by Noah's flood. On their journey, they must also have met the British leaders who were the prototypes of our legendary King Arthur. Both Arthur and the saints have left their mark firmly on the stories that have become attached to many of the places this walk passes through; those of the tinners have to be sought out more assiduously, although their imprint on the ground is just as obvious and far more authentic.

The walk starts at Tintagel, the site of an important Celtic monastery, where the Arthur industry is now at its silliest. It would be a pity to let the awfulness of that village high street in the summer season ruin the start of a good walk, so I advise taking the track up to the cliff and starting off from Tintagel church, rather than by visiting the castle along the tourist-ridden village street, which has nothing to commend it apart from the crosses marked on the stone which has stood in what is now the garden of the Warncliffe Arms Hotel since 1874, having been previously used for four years as a gatepost by a neighbouring farmer.

You can get to Tintagel church either by leaving

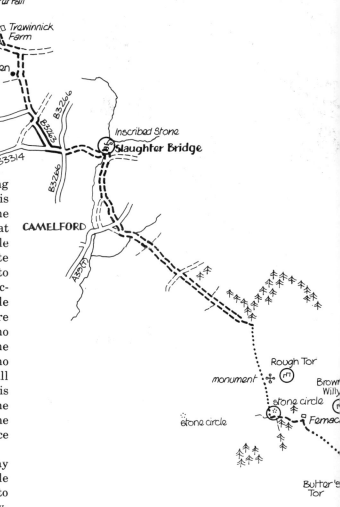

themum (they are imported and I can find no local name) need good drainage for their roots, and they find it between the slates which make up this part of the Cornish coast.

It is a pity, even in the tourist season, to come this way without visiting the castle, which was already in ruins when John Leland came here in 1538. 'It hath bene a marvelus strong and notable fortress,' he wrote, 'and almost *situ loci inexpug-*

the B3263 at Tregatta [200: 055874], or by braving the village and taking the left-hand lane which is signposted to the church. This lane runs past the vicarage where a small chapel is housed in what was once a stable block. The archway of the stable buildings frames the dome of a medieval dovecote in the vicarage garden. The chapel is dedicated to Our Lady of Fontevrault, for the French Benedictine Abbey which owned these lands in the Middle Ages. The church at the top of the lane has a more mysterious patron. Nobody knows for certain who St Materiana was, but she is thought to be the same person as St Madryn, a Welsh princess, who came across the channel to evangelize Cornwall about AD 500. The outside of the building is remarkable for the stone cattle grids at each of the two entrances to the churchyard, and for the stone coffin rest at the centre of the lych gate, which once incorporated a Roman milestone.

The path from the church runs a little way inland from the island on which Tintagel Castle stands above a cliff face covered from April to August with bright puce, daisy-like flowers growing out of succulent leaves. These mesembryan-

nabile especially for the donjon [keep] that is on this great high terrible cragge. But the residue of the buildinges of the castel be sore wether-beten and yn ruine.'

Geoffrey of Monmouth claimed that this was Arthur's palace and here, according to one Cornish legend, the great king died. That story gave rise to the superstition that twice a year the castle becomes invisible to common eyes, which, in the mists that haunt these coasts, it often does. On a clear day, any pure white gull of above average size soon hovering over the castle's island is said to be the spirit of Arthur bewailing the plight of Britain. This place is also held, in a tradition perpetuated by Matthew Arnold, to have been the capital of Mark, King of Cornwall, and husband of Iseult, whose tragic story really belongs to the southern part of this walk.

It is the ruins of the Celtic monastery on the eastern slopes of the crag that make this island promontory so well worth visiting. The cells on the terraces have been carefully marked out, and the monastery church and garden on the summit of the cliff are far more evocative of the life that was once lived here than are the ruins of the castle's defences. This monastery probably owed its existence to St Juliot, a Celtic missionary saint, and the importance of his foundation can be judged by the extent of the territory covered by its ruins.

To the east of the castle, the coastal path, flanked by thrift, white sea campion and foxgloves, climbs from headland to headland. It is a beautiful and dramatic walk in any weather, and the enchantment of the narrow Rocky Valley [200: 074895] makes a proper climax to the first stage of this route. This valley is reputed to be the last haunt of the scarlet-legged Cornish chough that became extinct in the early years of this century. Like those birds, the people have now left this valley, although it was certainly well inhabited for centuries, and probably for thousands of years. A little way inland from the coastal path are traces of the fields that were once cultivated by the people evangelized by the monks of Tintagel monastery.

Rocky Valley is narrow and wooded. By the small bridge which crosses the stream running through it there is a huddle of ruined buildings, the remains of a small worsted-weaving mill On the bare rock face behind them two labyrinths, cut in the form of a Cretan maze, have been carved. They have been attributed to some Bronze Age rite, but the cynical suggest that they could be the work of bored weavers. Whoever did them, and for whatever reason, they are beautiful things, and a good deal of skill and care must have gone into their making. It is happy that they have been preserved.

Inland from the mill is the Boscastle road and uphill to the east along the road the chapel of St Piran and the path to St Nectan's Glen and waterfall [200: 084886]. The left-hand lane by the chapel climbs past the entrances to some isolated houses to reach the glen and hermitage of St Nectan, restored in 1900 and now in decay again. There was once a tea garden set up in this spot, but it too has fallen into ruins. Like the setting of some mildly eerie film, in 1981 the rotting wooden tables still stood on the garden terrace outside the kitchen, whose door swung open to the weather. This recent ruin is much more desolate than the relics of Tintagel Castle, for very few people make their way to this unhappy garden. The fortunate ones who do find that a flight of winding, slippery steps go down to one of the best of waterfalls – a powerful stream rushing through a hole in the high rocks.

The walk continues with a climb back through the ruined tea garden and a scramble over some rather uneasy stepping stones. The lane to Camelford goes over the hill crowned by Condolden Barrow [200: 091872], a grassy mound topped by a triangulation point. It stands at the end of a wide path running north along the ridge towards Tintagel. The way to the south goes over Slaughterbridge

Brownwilly
Downs

Catshole
Tor

Tolborough
Tor

Priddacombe
Down

[200: 109855] where, according to some legends, Arthur received his fatal wound in a battle in which his treacherous nephew, Mordred, was also slain. There is a tradition, retold in M. A. Courtney's *Cornish Feasts and Folklore*, that all the time the king 'lay-a-dying, supernatural noises were heard in the castle, the sea and winds moaned, and their lamenting never ceased until our hero was buried at Glastonbury.'

A more likely source for the name of the fatal bridge is that it was the site of a great battle between the Britons and the Saxons which is supposed to have taken place here in 823. The two traditions can be related, however, if you believe, as I do, that Arthur was never one historical person, but a Celtic demi-god, whose mantel could fall on any heroic and actual Romano-British leader.

There is a trout farm on the eastern side of the bridge. A little way along the driveway leading to it there is a bungalow to the right. On the river bank beneath it, reached by a narrow public footpath, a large stone lies on its side in the mud. The inscription on it – *'Latinii acta Filius'* – is still easy to read, and suggests that it may have been a memorial to some Romanized Celtic soldier who fell in that late battle against the Saxons.

As far as this walk is concerned there is no need to go into Camelford, but the small but comprehensive private museum of Cornish life which is housed there is well worth a visit. The actual walk continues along the straight lane that goes southeast to Rough Tor [200: 145808], and which is signposted to the memorial to the 43rd Division of the Wessex Light Infantry. The tor, which lies on National Trust land, is memorial enough in itself, although a rough cross has been marked by the logan rock to the east of the summit, and an official commemorative plaque stands on the site where a medieval chapel dedicated to St Michael once stood.

The western slopes of the tor are covered with the small circular traces of a Bronze Age settlement; from its summit you can see two of the stone circles which were the ceremonial meeting places of the people who once lived here. This walk goes through the one that lies immediately beneath the tor [200: 145799]; the other, which is about a

mile to the west by the china clay workings [200: 125799], comes into Walk 11. That is to look forward to the new routes; looking east from Rough Tor's summit you can see ground you have already covered – the high ridges of Dartmoor, and the height of Kit Hill rearing out of the plain between these two granite uplands.

The two circles below Rough Tor, which date from the end of the third millennium BC, are among the earliest in the country. The one which gets its name from the nearest farm of Fernacre and lies in the path of this walk has a diameter of some 150 feet and contains fifty-two small granite stones whose complex alignments have been carefully studied by Professor Thom. The main entrance to the circle appears to have been on the northwest, facing the heights of Rough Tor. To the southeast there is an outrider on which the sunrise alignments are based; the stone stands in direct line to the highest point of Brown Willy [201: 158800] just to the east. A third circle (which is also a focal point of Walk 11) lies to the south. It is made up of the Stripple Stones [200: 144753] of Hawk's Tor. The surprising thing is that although the two other circles lie so near to Fernacre, they are all completely hidden from each other. G. F. Tregelles, a contributor to the *Victoria County History*, commenting on that fact remarked that the Fernacre circle was the pivot for the alignments for the other two.

The track that goes east to the deserted farm of Fernacre [201: 152798] enters the valley beneath Brownwilly Downs. By the stream below the farmhouse there is an extraordinary large boulder in what appears to be a stone wall. Closer investigation proves it to be a circular hut with a corbelled roof, as you can see if you follow the sheep which have obviously been here and crawl inside. The five courses of stone have been so fitted together as to form a perfect dome, leaving a hole from which the hearth smoke can escape. Even if this is not a complete Bronze Age dwelling, but simply a medieval pigsty or an even later herdsman's shelter, it is certainly built in a pattern that the worshippers at the stone circles would have understood. The Reverend Sabine Baring-Gould, who always went for the best of all possible (and

Hut circles,
Rough Tor

impossible) worlds, resolved the matter for himself by declaring that it certainly was a Bronze Age dwelling, 'spared because the farmer thought it might serve his purpose as a pigsty or a butter house'.

The course of this walk along the valley beneath Brown Willy goes by several other settlements of hut circles, but none are so satisfying as this one building at Fernacre. The way down the valley is marshy and has to be dealt with carefully; the bogs here are as treacherous as those of Dartmoor. 'Places to which you hardly desire to consign your worst enemies,' wrote Baring-Gould, adding with most unclerical glee, 'always excepting promoters of certain companies, I really should enjoy seeing them flounder there.'

Brown Willy at nearly 1400 feet is the highest hill in Cornwall, hence its name which is derived from the Celtic *bryn geled*, a conspicuous hill. The long stretch of its shoulder, although it lacks the dramatic rocky castellations of Rough Tor, towers grandly above the valley. On the southern slopes of Brownwilly Downs this walk leaves the marshes to climb round Catshole Tor [201: 168785] and over Priddacombe Down to the farm track [201: 173772] from which a field path runs to the back entrance of Jamaica Inn, made famous by Daphne du Maurier's novel of that name and now a crowded tourist spot. Its popularity is fairly recent, for visitors at the end of the nineteenth century had to be warned that this was a temperance house.

The way south goes by the farm track [201: 179762] over Minzies Downs to Dozmary

Walk 8 Saints and Tinners

Pool [201: 195745], a place more dramatic in legend than in actuality, for what the visitor finds is a flat grey sheet of water fringed by soggy reeds. On a grey day it must be one of the most depressing places in England, yet it is a fairly sheltered spot and was once the home of the earliest settlers in Cornwall. Mesolithic flints in some number have been found along its shores, which are protected by high ground from the easterly winds.

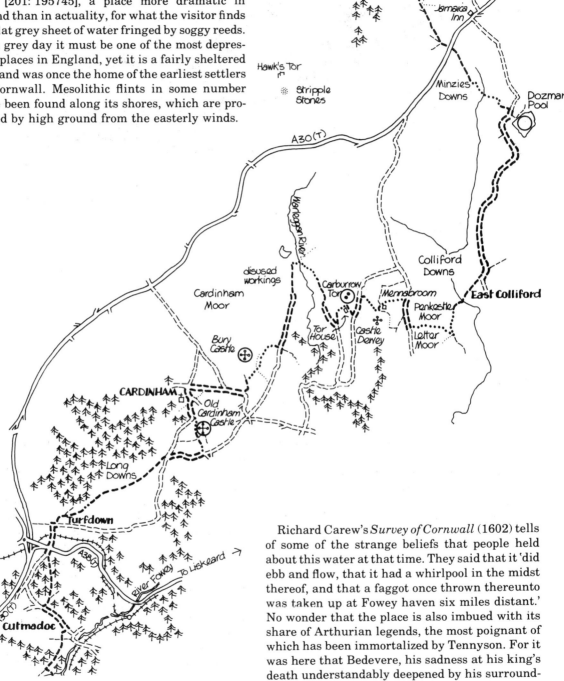

Richard Carew's *Survey of Cornwall* (1602) tells of some of the strange beliefs that people held about this water at that time. They said that it 'did ebb and flow, that it had a whirlpool in the midst thereof, and that a faggot once thrown thereunto was taken up at Fowey haven six miles distant.' No wonder that the place is also imbued with its share of Arthurian legends, the most poignant of which has been immortalized by Tennyson. For it was here that Bedevere, his sadness at his king's death understandably deepened by his surround-

Dozmary Pool

ings, had to return three times before he could bring himself to carry out his master's commands and hurl the sword Excalibur into the waters from which it had emerged. It is harder to imagine the retrieving arm, 'clothed in white samite, mystic, wonderful', breaking the sluggish surface of these waters.

The story that Dozmary Pool was the scene of the awful drudgery imposed on the ghost of the tyrannical Jan Tregeagle seems more appropriate to the place. That spirit was doomed to bail out these supposedly bottomless waters with a cracked limpet shell, until he was sent by St Petroc to sweep the sands of the Looe estuary. Far from being bottomless, the pool is actually so shallow that they say you can wade across it, although I have not put that to the test. As for Jan Tregeagle, there is a tradition, probably spurious, that identifies him with the John Tregeagle who died in 1679, and who lies in Treworder churchyard.

From Dozmary Pool, the way goes south and

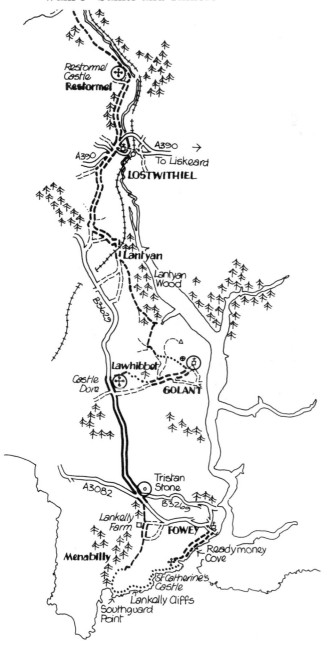

west across the downs towards Carburrow Tor [201: 155708]. This hill is surmounted by two barrows which are believed by tradition to contain the bodies of two kings buried in golden coffins. Perhaps that story arose from the careful siting of these barrows, which indicates at least that people of great importance were buried there.

From that tor the walk goes across the Warleggan river to Cardinham Moor [200: 135715]. All around this way there is evidence of the old tin workings. When Murray's *Handbook* was compiled in 1859, the contributor on this part of Bodmin Moor noted that the ancient workings at Treveddoc in the parish of Warleggan were 'still in activity, and having in addition to the excavations of the streamers, shafts 60 fath. deep, which are said to have been sunk by "the old men".' The latter were those who worked and then abandoned the mines centuries before.

The walk leaves the southern edge of the moor to go past two ancient fortifications: the earthworks of the castle of Cardinham [200: 126680] and the much-restored fortress of Restormel [200: 105614]. Between the two, the countryside is pleasantly wooded; the walk goes past the Lanyhdrock Nature Trail and for the last mile or so it takes you along the banks of the river Fowey.

Restormel Castle, which is now in the care of the Department of the Environment, was first built on an existing earthwork and bailey by the Norman, Baldwin Fitz Turstin, at the beginning of the twelfth century, on a site that is a natural choice for anyone wanting to secure this territory from invaders by land or river. The keep, which lay in ruins by the seventeenth century, was none the less used as a garrison during the Civil War when it sheltered soldiers of Lord Essex's parliamentarian army. It was captured by Sir Richard Grenville in 1644. The outer skeleton of the building has now been almost overpreserved, so that the whole castle, on its smooth, symmetrical mound, seems like a textbook reconstruction of a model Norman fortification.

From Restormel, the road goes by the ancient Stannary town of Lostwithiel, and then, before reaching Fowey, turns aside to pick up the threads of the Arthurian romance at the church of St

Sampson at Golant [200: 121552]. Here, as legend has it, King Mark and Iseult used to worship, until she fell in love with Tristan and their tragedy began. As for the saint, he was among those who crossed Cornwall on his way from Wales to Brittany. As he passed through the peninsula he stopped to found a church here as well as another at Southill near Callington. According to Celtic law, in order to do that he had to stay on each site for forty days, existing on one simple meal each day and only varying his diet by the addition of an egg on Sundays. His time was spent in prayer and supplication for the people of the neighbourhood.

From Golant, the walk turns to another great earthwork, the banks of Castle Dore [200: 104548], which has a more direct connection with Arthur, for it is said to have been the palace of Gorlais, whose wife, Igraine, was raped by his murderer, Uther. From that unholy alliance, Arthur was conceived. Historically the 'castle', which was first built around 200 BC, was restored and occupied until the sixth century AD. The earthworks that can be seen today are unusual in having an inner ring that is 7 feet higher than the outer. Excavations have revealed that at one time an elaborate timber gateway stood at its eastern entrance; other finds from the site are now housed in the museum at Truro.

Most likely it was the occupants of Castle Dore who arranged that a stone should be erected to mark the spot of Tristan's burial in AD 550. The stone still exists, standing very near its original position on the eastern side of the crossroads [200: 109525] just outside Fowey. It is inscribed 'Drustans hic iacet Cunomori filius'. That Cunomorus is another name for Mark, and the stone puts a sinister twist to Tristan's tragedy.

This walk finishes as it began, along a coastal path. The farm track that runs south from the Tristan Stone takes you to fields which go down to the sea at Southground Point. To the west are the woods of Menabilly, which Daphne du Maurier immortalized as Mandalay, and the swans swimming in the calm waters of Polridmouth. To the east the path goes up to Lankelly Cliffs which are surmounted by corn fields and where the path is strewn with scarlet pimpernel. This coastal path

is infinitely more gentle than that above the slate cliffs of the north. Yet this shore has its own dramatic quality, enhanced by the cormorants fishing from its rocks. The path goes past the earthworks of St Catherine's Castle [200: 115509] at the head of the Fowey estuary, and so to Readymoney Cove. From here you can either go through the National Trust property of Covington Woods with its romantic mossed ruins, or make directly for the town of Fowey. It was from this place, and from St Blaizey to the west, which was also once a sea port, that the saints set sail for Brittany and where the tinners came to exchange their goods with men from all over Europe and the Near East. Although that trade started many centuries before the saints brought their Christian message, the tinners were not the first to make use of the estuary. Around 3000 BC, the people from northwest France, who were going to settle on Bodmin Moor, arrived here in their frail crafts.

Castle Dore

Walk 9
More Saints' Roads

The course of this walk lies along the coast to the northwest of the moor. I have included it here partly because of the obvious glory of this stretch of shore, and partly because it traverses many of the paths trodden by the Welsh and Irish saints who founded Christian cells here before journeying across to Brittany.

The walk starts, however, along that stretch of the newly formed north Cornwall coastal path which runs along the cliff top from Tintagel church to Port Gaverne [200: 003819] on the inlet just to the east of Port Isaac. You must allow at least four hours to cover this distance, although from the start it looks as if there is only a very short way to go, for from the cliff heights Port Isaac appears to be very close. There is nothing to indicate how slippery and difficult the path is going to be, and how steeply it climbs up and down the intervening headlands. On no account try to do this walk in a mist; if you should be caught in one, head inland as soon as you can, for you must not be lulled into the feeling that a Countryside Commission long-distance path carries any guarantee of security. This one runs very close to the cliff edge, and that cliff is crumbling.

There are no cliff castles on this stretch of headland, but the walk starts by going past a group of tumuli, and then passes a bleak brick-built lookout tower at Jacket's Point [200: 034831]. That marks the halfway point of this part of the walk, which ends where the lane runs into Port Isaac.

To get to Plain Street [200: 976786] you can either take the field path by Trewinte, or the lanes to St Endellion [200: 996786]. Where the lane enters that village, you will see two long stone pillars – the remains of crosses – from which the Long Cross Inn takes its name. The church is dedicated to St Endelentia, who lived in the sixth

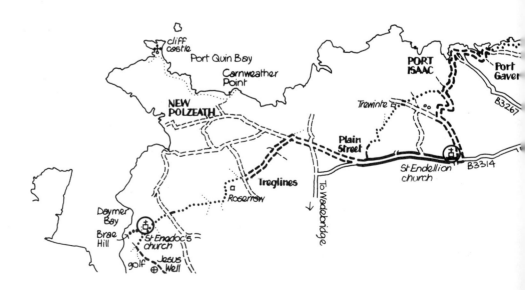

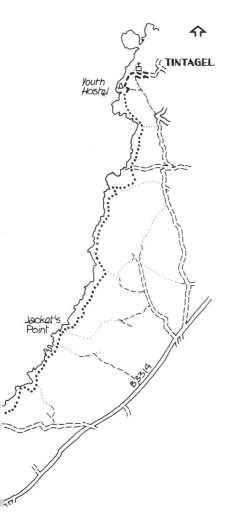

century and who is said to have been a god-daughter of King Arthur's. She is supposed to have been buried on this site, which became a collegiate church for a small colony of priests in the early thirteenth century.

The legends of this saint make her daughter to the Welsh king Brychan, and sister to St Udy, St Teatch and to many other holy women to whom

churches in the neighbourhood are dedicated. It is unlikely that anyone ever meant to imply that all these ladies were really blood sisters. It is far more likely, indeed very probable, that they all came together as a missionary order, landing perhaps at Tintagel, where they made the Celtic monastery a first base.

St Endelentia herself is said to have finally settled a little to the south of the village which now bears her name, and to have lived solely on the milk of a single cow. One day this cow strayed into the land of the Lord of Trentinney, who killed the animal, whereupon King Arthur slew him. Endelentia immediately used her holy gifts to restore the tyrant to life. I do not know what happened to the cow, but this was not the end of her reliance on animals. Before she died she asked that her corpse should be put on a cart pulled by bullocks or one-year-old heifers. She requested that they bury her at the place where these beasts stopped. A picture of the dead saint lying on the ox-cart is among the other figures of Cornish saints painted by Newlyn artists for the church of St Hilary, which is visited in Walk 15.

Her story is not uncommon: the last resting place of many saints is discovered by beasts. I found a very similar tale in East Anglia and concluded then that this folk tale is linked to a distant memory of the way most old roads were first blazed by animals. The saints in general are often credited with being much more sensitive to the instincts that guide animal movements than the rest of us are.

From St Endelentia's ground the walk goes along the lanes to New Polzeath [200: 935797], whose headland has been mercifully saved from caravan sites by the National Trust, and whose Cliff Castle stands at the most northerly point, a formidable fortress guarding the entrance to Port Quin Bay to the east and the Camel estuary to the west. This must have been Petroc's landfall as he sailed into Cornwall.

A lesser saint to come this way was Enedoc. The church [200: 932773] which bears his name was restored in 1863. It is still almost hidden by the surrounding sand dunes, but at one time it was completely covered, earning it the local name of

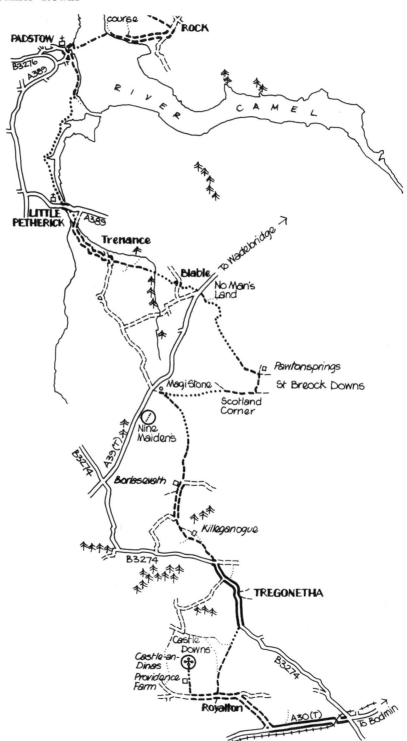

Sinkinnery church. In those days a service was held there only once a year; there was no congregation and the officiating cleric had to be let in through the skylight, a feat of acrobatics that kept his stipend going.

Little is known about that early sunken building, but one of the bells which was sold to defray the expense of the nineteenth-century restoration was actually inscribed 'Alfredus Rex', and is thought to date from the ninth century. The churchyard was originally oval, which probably indicates a Celtic origin, and although the earliest tombs in it are from the fifteenth century, third- and fourth-century Celtic remains have been found among the dunes. There was a sizable Iron Age settlement on Brae Hill [200: 929772] nearby.

It is a church that Sir John Betjeman knows, for both his parents loved this church and his mother is buried here. His poem on the Sunday afternoon services at St Enedoc's tells of 'the lady's finger, thyme/And bright varieties of saxifrage' which grow beside the paths running through the dunes. They are still there.

According to the Reverend William Henry, a recent vicar of the parish, St Enedoc was a hermit who lived in a cave on the site of the present church, having chosen to settle near the spring, which was discovered when the flagstones by the rood screen were found to be continually damp after the nineteenth-century restoration.

From the church you can climb up to Brae Hill to the north of the golf course, where tumuli mark the site of the ancient settlement which later became a Roman camp. Long before that time, anyone looking west from this hilltop would not have seen the waters of Daymer Bay, which now lie beneath it, for they cover a great forest of oaks, yews and hazel, whose stumps and roots were discovered in 1857 when a gale of unusual force shifted the sand at low tide.

The track that runs southeast alongside the golf course is marked out by white stones. The banks of the streams here are full of yellow flags and purple orchids; and although I did not see the 'Red Admirals basking with their wings apart' which Sir John noted in his poem, the place was alive with small blue butterflies when I was there early

in June. To the right of the path is the Jesus Well [200: 936765] where St Enedoc is supposed to have baptized his converts. A baptistry dating from the fifteenth century stands over the well, whose waters were supposed to have the power to cure whooping cough.

From Rock you have to take a ferry across the mouth of the Camel to St Petroc's settlement at Padstow, where St Patrick is said to have stayed while he was on his mission to Cornwall. The contributor to Murray's *Handbook* found it 'one of those antiquated, unsavoury fishing-towns, which are viewed most agreeably from a distance'. That could still be true during the summer when the place is filled with tourists who find such places quaint and unwittingly destroy their genuine life. But even the thousands of visitors cannot completely swamp the integrity of Padstow's great festival, the May Day processions of the rival hobby horses.

This pagan fertility rite, whose origins are now a matter for speculation, is kept alive today by two processions, each one claiming prime authenticity, and each one centred on the prancing figure of a hobby horse, an elaborate frame (culminating in an articulated jaw) which covers two men. These creatures symbolize both the energy of the sun and the fertility of the earth, and their dance through the streets is part of the sympathetic magic that was intended to ensure the successful growth of crops and beasts in the coming summer.

I find it best to go to Padstow in winter, when the fishing boats are pulled up in the harbour, and the two ' 'osses' are safely stabled in their respective inns. As far as I know, no one has thought of reviving the old game that used to be played here by the tinners on St Paul's Day (25 January). The game went on up to the middle of the last century, and simply consisted of pelting a large water pitcher with stones until it was quite demolished. Presumably this was a relic of some early rite connected with the solstice, but its origins have long been lost. Perhaps Petroc even put a temporary end to both summer and winter rituals when he founded his monastery here in the sixth century.

The present church at Padstow dates from the

fifteenth century, but it still bears marks of the monastic settlement that Petroc founded here. Outside the south door is a four-holed Celtic cross, from which the saint and his predecessors preached to their flocks; and by the southeast gateway a massive faintly-carved stone stump is thought to be the remains of the cross which once stood inside the monastery gateway.

The walk out of Padstow goes past Petroc's later settlement in the valley where the village of Little Petherick is now. This is the scene of a haunting described by Michael Williams of Bossiney in his book *The Supernatural in Cornwall*. One explanation put forward for the appearance of the ghost which took the form of a small grey-robed figure, was that it was seen on a stretch of the lane that was reported to be the old priests' road from Padstow to Bodmin.

This walk does not follow that, but makes for even more mysterious country, St Breock Downs to the south of Wadebridge. Here we leave the realm of Celtic saints and enter the holy places of the Bronze Age, for the ridgeway path across the downs is marked out by tumuli and burial chambers. From Scotland Corner [200: 948684], a wide farm track goes to the great standing stone which is aligned to the only stone row in Cornwall. These stones stand beside the hedge, a field away from the A39(T). The row extends about 350 feet, and as each stone is nearly 6 feet tall, they are much higher than those of the Dartmoor rows. As this row was probably set up during the Bronze Age, it must already have become a place of superstitious awe rather than religious reverence by the time St Petroc came to preach the gospel here.

Although the row is called the Nine Maidens, I counted ten stones, two of which have fallen. One of these may be an interloper, but in any case the word 'nine' does not simply signify a number. Many stone circles and clumps of barrows throughout the country attract that numeral, no matter how many stones are actually present. B. C. Spooner's explanation is that all these 'nine' circles and rows are associated with 'noon' or 'nones', the midday canonical hour, when the stones are supposed to have bowed to the sun – a memory of the part they originally played in solar rites.

From these stones, the walk ends by going from Bronze Age to Iron Age, crossing Tregonetha Downs to Providence and climbing to the three-ringed hill fort of Castle-an-Dinas [200: 945625], which extends over six acres, and which King Arthur is supposed to have used as a hunting lodge. When it was originally built in the second or first century BC, huts stood in the inner ramparts, and the well that served the people who dwelt here is still visible as a marshy pool. There is no doubt that the prime function of this fort was to guard the routes of the tin traders, for many deposits have been found around it.

Castle an Dinas

Walk 10

The Tinners' Way to the East

Throughout the Stone Age, axes from the green-stone axe factories near St Ives and Penzance were traded throughout the country. Those that went to East Anglia were probably paid for in flints from Grimes Graves. Later the tin from the granite of Penwith and Bodmin Moor went right through the south of England on its way to the Continent. The traders must have gone along a route which is mostly covered by the present A30. This walk which runs on either side of that highway divides into two parts, the first and shorter section simply going from Bodmin town through Cardinham [200: 124688] to join the A30 some 3 miles east of Jamaica Inn.

Bodmin, which has always been the largest town in Cornwall, grew up on the site where St Petroc is said to have founded his monastery in the middle of the sixth century. He was the son of a Welsh king and went to Ireland before crossing into Cornwall. His Bodmin church was rebuilt in the fifteenth century when the town appears to have had a population of some three thousand and boasted forty trade guilds. The other great church in the town belonged to the Franciscans, who were disbanded in the Reformation following the Pilgrimage of Grace. Their church, which survived until the nineteenth century, stood where the Assize Court is now. Today, Bodmin's centre is a pleasing, spacious place, one of its greatest resources for the visitor being the bookshop run by Pat Munn, historian and specialist on Cornish lore, whose stock must be among the most comprehensive collections of West Country books.

From Bodmin the walk goes by Callywith [200: 089684] and the track through the woods to the site of Old Cardinham Castle [200: 126680]. The earthworks of this fortification stand a little to the south of the site of a Norman castle, which was destroyed in the fourteenth century, although traces of its motte and bailey can be seen from the lane going to Cardinham church.

There is an army rifle range on the moor to the north of that village, so if the danger flag is flying, you must take the lanes to Maidenwell [200: 145707] instead of going across the open moor to that point. That need not prevent you from climbing to the Iron Age fort of Bury Castle [200: 135696] before crossing the Warleggan river to the east of the old china clay works and going over the moor to Coppins Park [201: 161730] and the main road.

Here the first part of the walk ends; the second starts at Jamaica Inn. The most notable thing to look out for, should you feel up to walking along the verge of this busy thoroughfare, is Fourhole Cross [201: 172750]. This is one of the oldest crosses on the moor. Its limbs were originally surrounded by a circle of stone, but as the top arch is missing, it now only has two holes.

The walk starts from the same field path at the back of the inn that we follow in Walk 8 (see page 73), then goes east along the lane which runs below the barrow on the height of Tolborough Tor [201: 175779] to the old farmhouse of Codda [201: 180784] sheltering in the lea of Codda Tor. From the footpath which goes from there across West Moor and Carne Down to Tresmeak [201: 209821], a divergence can be made to Leskernick Hill [201: 184804] to the north, or to Elephant Rock [201: 195791] on the slopes of Hendra Downs to the south.

The isolated farmhouse of Leskernick was occupied until the mid-1960s. It shelters beneath the bare rounded summit of Leskernick Hill. In contrast to that rockless height, the oddly balanced glacial stones that form Elephant Rock stand to the south of the path on the slopes of Hendra Beacon. On Carne Down the footpath becomes a track running to Tresmeak and the lanes and field paths that lead to St Clether. Just below the church there is a footpath running along the eastern slopes of the Inny valley.

Here, in a romantic pastoral setting in a field which used to be known as Chapel Park, gentle despite its rocks and contrasting strangely with the stark, harsh grandeur of the moor, St Clether's Well [201: 204848] is to be found, with a little chapel standing on the slope beside it. Inside the chapel, which was reconstructed in the fifteenth century, stands a stone altar. It has not been moved since the early Christians put it there in the sixth century.

During the late medieval reconstruction, the water from the holy well was channelled through the building, running behind the altar and emerging again through the southern wall, whose outer side has a small shelf for the pilgrims' thanks offerings. The water was supposed to have healing properties, and is indeed still used for baptisms in the parish church. Like most Cornish saints, St Clether was a Welshman, the son of a prince of Carmarthen. He lived in this valley for many years during the sixth century, and is believed to have died near Liskeard.

The restored chapel, in its turn, gradually fell into ruins through disuse, and when Baring-Gould took over the supervision of its rebuilding in the 1890s, he found it in a 'condition of complete ruin; almost every stone was prostrate and the rebuilding was like the putting together of a

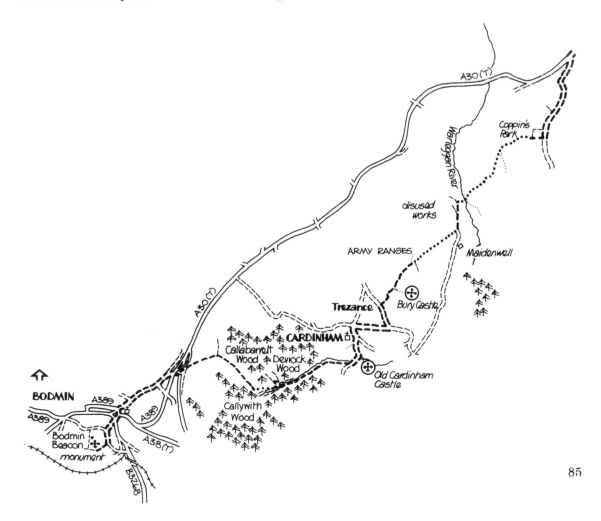

Bridge at Altarnun

child's puzzle.' When he finally succeeded in re-assembling it, he discovered that the fifteenth-century planners had acted according to the vision described in the first verse of Ezekiel 47: 'After-ward he brought me again unto the door of the house; and behold, waters issued out from under the threshold of the house eastward; for the fore-front of the house stood toward the east and waters came down from under the right side of the house, at the south side of the altar.'

From this little chapel, the path continues northwest along the valley until it reaches the lane leading to the A395 for Launceston, where this walk properly ends. However, St Clether is a good starting point for an exploration of the north-east section of the moor, and so I have added a

coda to this walk which goes to North Hill [201: 273766]. To take this walk, retrace your steps to Tresmeak, and then make for the village of Altarnun [201: 224814], whose name derives either from the altar of St Non or Nonna, the mother of St David, or more prosaically from the cliffs which took that saint's name.

From there the best way to get onto the moor is by the farm of Treburland [201: 235794] and the path which climbs up to Nine Stones. These are the remains of a stone circle, restored to its present state by a past landowner, who is reported to have thought that nine was the appropriate number of stones for such old monuments, a re-addition aris-ing, as we have seen, from the confusion between 'nones' or 'noon' and the number nine.

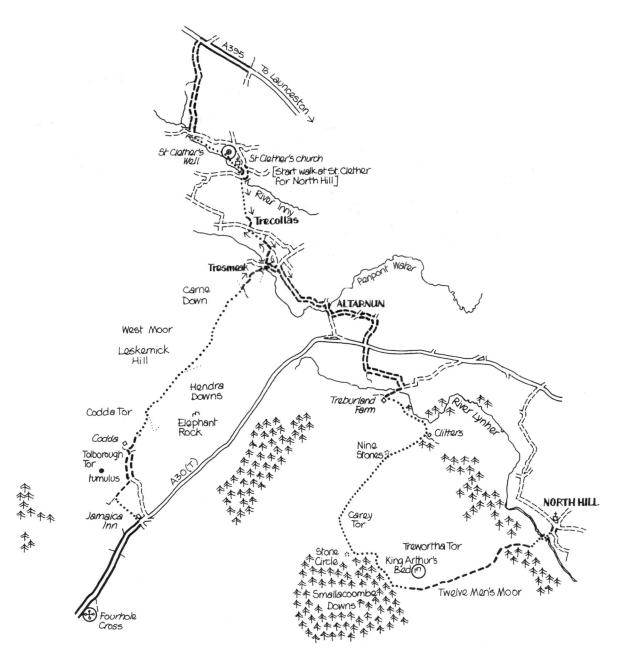

Bodmin

From the circle the route goes southwest over Carey Tor to another stone circle [201: 226760] on the edge of the conifer forest of Smallacoombe Down, and from there it turns south by the rock of King Arthur's Bed [201: 242757] on Trewortha Tor. This is a large rock basin, caused by the erosion of the rock surface by small particles of stone being swirled by wind and rain within an existing depression. It has a separate circular hollow in which one could imagine a human head resting, while the body lay in the remainder of the basin. This forms the 'bed', but I can find no record of its association with Arthur, although it fits in well with the many natural and manmade wonders of the moor which have been absorbed into his legend.

From the rock a track which was a well-used drove road for centuries, and along which sheep and cattle were brought to their summer pastures by Trewortha Farm, runs to the east. The stretch of country through which it passes is known as Twelve Men's Moor, and gets its name from an agreement on grazing rights made in 1284 between the Prior of Launceston on the one hand, and William of Trewortha and eleven tenant farmers on the other. They were bound to give some services to the priory and had to pay an annual rent of four shillings each Michaelmas. Around Trewortha Farm there are traces of the medieval hamlet where the herdsmen and their families lived during the summer months.

The walk, which goes to the eastern edge of the moor, ends with a steep descent along a hollow way running through a wood. The stream at the bottom is crossed by a wooden bridge, and on the other side of it a field path leads into the lane opposite North Hill church.

Walk 11
The Pattern of the Circles

In 1898, at a time when Sabine Baring-Gould was busy investigating the archaeological sites of Cornwall and Dartmoor, the *Journal of the Royal Institute of Cornwall* published an article by a Mr A. R. Lewis, in which he traced the alignments of the stone circles in the northwest of Bodmin Moor. This walk follows the course of his observations and provides a chance to look at those circles, all of which appear to have been constructed during the latter part of the second millennium BC, and at one even more inexplicable relic. The way starts by going west along the lanes from Blisland church [200: 100732] to Manor Common, and along the farm track that runs beside the outrider of the first circle to be visited.

The Trippet Stones [200: 132750], as this circle is called, lie a little to the north, clearly visible from the road. There are only eight standing stones left now, but each one has a height of at least 4 feet. On the ground beside them lie four of their fallen comrades. A dozen more stones probably went to the make up of the original circle, but they have disappeared, no doubt to be used in farm buildings throughout the centuries.

The Bronze Age men who met here would have known the cheesewring-shaped stones of Carbilly Tor to the north, and looking west to the ridge of Hawk's Tor they could see the splendour of the Stripple Stones [200: 144753]. As John Aubrey said of Avebury and Stonehenge, that more magnificent circle stands in relation to the Trippet Stones as a cathedral does to a parish church.

These two circles stand on opposite sides of a valley and are the only two on the moor which are visible to each other, although from every circle in this group of alignments it is possible to see Rough Tor. The way to Hawk's Tor goes across the stream dividing the circles by the track that runs to the northwest of the farm. It goes through a gate and across a few stepping stones, which only serve in dry weather. From this point you can look back to see the Trippet Stones standing impressively on the skyline.

The whole of the climb up to Hawk's Tor, although it goes along a well-used track, or perhaps because it does, is very muddy. Its saving grace in October is that it then becomes the haunt of golden plovers. The Stripple Stones are along the ridge from the rocks of Hawk's Tor and not immediately visible from the heights. When you reach them you will discover the most complex sacred site on the moor, although this fact is obscured by the swamp which surrounds the remaining stones. This has come about because the original circle was enclosed by a bank and a ditch, which was once 9 feet wide and 3 feet deep. As at Avebury, the earthen bank was thrown up outside the ditch, showing that the former was not part of a fortification, but served as a promenading gallery from which people could watch the rituals enacted on the platform on which the stones stood.

It is not possible to conjecture what religious or political ceremonies they watched, or what the original structure was like. Only fifteen stones in an irregular circle, and a further three seemingly at random within the enclosure, remain of that forgotten splendour. Lewis found that a direct line north from here went through Garrow Tor [200: 145785] and the Fernacre circle [200: 145799], which also stands on an alignment from the Trippet Stones, and so to Rough Tor. He believed that this sighting to the north would be especially significant to the people gathered at the Stripple Stones henge, for over the rocks of the tor they would see the seven stars of the Great Bear pointing to the Pole Star.

This walk does not follow that line directly, but goes northwest of Carkees Tor to approach the

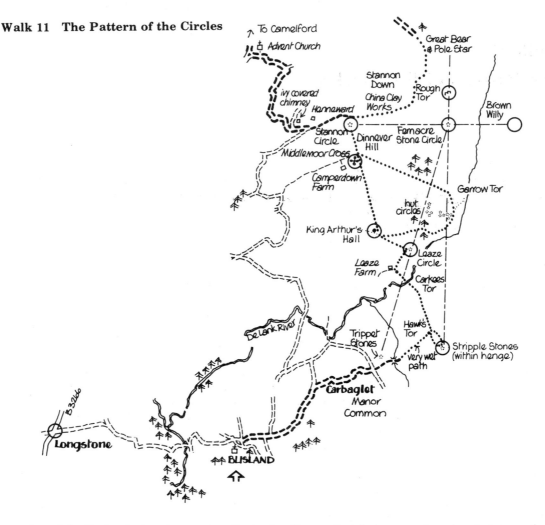

crossing of the De Lank river by a series of ruined and ancient farm buildings. The river's name is not of Norman origin; 'De' comes from the Celtic *dhu*, black. Its stream is clear enough, but this whole area, despite the practical workings of the waterboard, which has a station here, is dark and mysterious. Across the river, to the north of the gate leading to the waterworks, is Leaze Farm house [200: 135768], one of the oldest on the moor. It is empty now, but although the dwelling is deserted, the moor around it has been extensively cultivated or turned to pasture land in several places.

Yet there is still a wide section of Emblance Downs that is in a rough natural state and only grazed by herds of ponies. The circle [200: 137774], which takes its name from the farm, is almost hidden by a small hill, and so little account has been taken of it in times past that a field bank runs diametrically across it. Lewis showed that this circle stands in a direct alignment with the Trippet Stones and the circle at Fernacre, although both are hidden from it. However, the rocks at Garrow Tor are visible from here, and Lewis discovered that anyone standing at the centre of the Leaze circle at midsummer would see the sun rise behind them.

This walk does not climb directly up to Garrow

Tor, but turning northwest to cross Emblance Downs, it visits King Arthur's Hall [200: 129777]. This mysterious rectangular pit, lined with granite slabs and some 30 by 50 yards in area, is sometimes described as a Bronze Age cattle pound, but its true nature has never been ascertained. The entrance is on the northeast corner facing Garrow Tor and the hut circles which shelter beneath it. The people who lived there either drove their cattle here, or used the construction for some ceremony that could not be performed at the stone circles. Perhaps they put it to both uses. Safeguarded from today's grazing animals by an enclosing fence, it is now still much as John Norden found it in 1584, 'situate on a playne Mountayne, wroughted some 3 foote into the grounde; and by reason of the depression of the place, there standeth a stange or Poole of water, the place sett rounde with flatt stones.'

From this mysterious monument you can either go directly northwest across the downs to Middlemoor Cross [200: 125794], or you can take a zigzag way by going east to Garrow Tor, from which height you can see both the Leaze circle and the one at Fernacre. Middlemoor Cross, which stands just to the east of Camperdown Farm, is the most remote of the Bodmin crosses. Tradition has it that it turned so often to the sound of St Breward church bells that eventually it fell down. The Stannon circle [200: 125798] on the other side of Dinnever Hill is to the north of the place where it now stands upright. An alignment from that circle runs due east through the Fernacre circle (see page 72), which is hidden from it by a slight rise in the ground, and so on to the heights of Brown Willy. Lewis showed that this line points to the equinoctal sunrise.

The two circles of Stannon and Fernacre are fairly similar. They are both flattened circles, with a maximum diameter of just under 150 feet. Both

Stannon stone circle

Stannon Stone Circle

seem to have had about sixty stones projecting about 3½ feet above the ground. At Stannon forty-one stones are still standing, and another lies fallen in the centre of the circle. Beside this ancient monument, whose stones mingle with the grazing sheep, are the startling white mounds of a china clay works, with the even more startling metallic blue of the water that has collected there. To reach Camelford from here, you can either make your way eastwards towards Rough Tor by way of Stannon Downs, or you can take the lanes going west by the tall ivy-covered chimney of an old mine by the farm of Henneward, and the isolated church of Advent [200: 105816].

Some say this much restored and renovated fifteenth-century building, which retains a delightful carved wooden face in its porch, gets its name from Adwen, the fourth-century son of a Welsh king who came here with his saintly sisters, Arianwen and Julitta. They must have been among the first of the evangelists to visit Cornwall. A more prosaic explanation is that it comes from the season of its original consecration.

Whatever its origin, for all its remoteness it is set in a gentle countryside, contrasting beautifully with the harsh moorland to the east and south of it where the circle builders set out their inexplicable alignments.

Part Three Penwith

Focal Points

NB: All references relate to Sheet 203

Ballowall Barrow 355313
Blind Fiddler 416282
Boscawen-noon Circle 413274
Bowl Rock 523368
Caer Brân 407290
Carn Brea 385280
Carn Euny 402289
Castle-an-Dinas 484351
Chûn Castle 405339
Chûn Quoit 402340
Chysauster 473350
Ding Dong Mine 435347
Drift Stones 436273
Kerris Roundago 442274
Lanyon Quoit 430337
Madron Well 445327
Maen Castle 348258
Mên-an-tol 427349
Mên Scryfa 429354
Merry Maidens 435246
Mulfra Quoit 452354
Nine Maidens 434353
Pipers 435248
St Credan's Well, Sancreed 420295
St Michael's Mount 515298
St Piran, Perranuthnoe 537295
Trereen Dinas 433387
Trencrom Hill Fort 518363
Tresvennack Pillar 442268
Zennor Quoit 469380

Part Three Penwith

Wind out of Cornwall, wind, if I forget:
Not in the tunnelled streets, where scarce men
 breathe
The air they live by, but wherever seas
Blossom in foam, wherever merchant bees
Volubly traffic upon any heath:
If I forget, shame me! or if I find
A wind in England like my Cornish wind.

                    Arthur Symons, 'Cornish Wind'

It comes as something of a shock to discover that
Arthur Symons, poet of the *Yellow Book* and
urbane darling of the decadent 1890s, should
revert over and over again to the Cornwall of his
childhood. He was born of Cornish parents and
although he only spent a few years of his childhood
in his native county (his father being a Wesleyan
minister, the family were constantly on the move),
he was brought up in the West Country and went
to school in Bideford.

Yet it was the few years he spent at St Ives that
imprinted the sea on his imagination, and it was to
Land's End, where he felt 'secure and alone like a
bird in a cleft of a rock', that he returned as a
famous, much-travelled and troubled man.

It was a solace denied to John Wesley, for when
he went to the edge of the promontory in September 1743 he found it 'an awful sight', and he
meant that word in its true meaning, for he
piously trusted that the scene below him would
'melt away when God ariseth in judgement. The
sea beneath does indeed boil like a pot. One would
think the deep to be hoary. But though they swell
yet can they not prevail, He shall set these bounds
which they cannot pass' – pseudo-Biblical language, which the writer and naturalist, W. H.
Hudson, another early twentieth-century visitor
to the far west of Cornwall, did not hesitate to pass
judgement on (*The Land's End*, 1908).

Old tin mine,
Botallok

This place, where the land narrows to the sea,
still exercises a curious hold on the people who
spend any time here, whether like Symons they
can boast that 'Bone by bone, blood by blood/I am a
Cornishman', or whether they are locally labelled
'grockles' or 'emmetts', visitors from across the
Tamar. Not every one likes this last moor of
Cornwall, but no one can be indifferent to it. It
weaves a fascination which cannot even be
quenched by the hordes of holidaymakers to Penzance at the height of season, by the ugly villas
and bungalows which they rent, or the shanty-

broker, Thomas Spargo, in *The Mines of Cornwall* (1865) explained how the Lord had favoured this small area with such great mineral wealth, and how it was almost a religious duty on the part of shareholders to invest in enterprises which would increase their money tenfold every year; especially as these mines were worked by 'some of the best men in England, engaged many hundreds of feet below the waves of the Atlantic, in carrying tunnels into the tin and copper lodes under the sea.' He goes on:

> How monotonous their lot, early in the morning, in the mid-day, and at midnight, you may find troops of these worthy labourers quietly and lovingly going to their underground labour, as if no other work had charms for them; the chorus to the stroke of their hammer, the echo of the sound of its blow, and above them the roar of the waves of the ocean as it traverses its yellow bed of granite sand, alone companion them; they fulfil their destiny with a patience and hopefulness that foreshadows constant good to the future of the human race.

In the course of walking through the old mining villages of this area, it is possible to discover how some of these sentimentally eulogized miners of a hundred years ago were rewarded for their toil.

It would not be fair to be too hard on Spargo and his friends, however, for the promontory which he described as 'the most remarkable land in England' has always attracted its exploiters. The classical writers who knew Penwith as the chief source of tin called it Belerion; and Milton modified that name in 'Lycidas' for Bellerus, the giant of Land's End. Certainly fierce giants were needed to protect the wealth of the tin, for before the Irish brought the Gospel to Cornwall, they came as plundering tyrants, and the fighting was so fierce

town airport of St Just. The scatter of tall chimneys and old industrial workings left over from the tin mining which flourished here intermittently from the Bronze Age to the early years of the nineteenth century only enhances the enchantment of the moorland which stretches from coast to coast.

Although the tinners left their marks all over Dartmoor and Bodmin, it is here, in Penwith, that the old mine workings are most dramatically obtrusive. With sickening complacency the nineteenth-century mining engineer and stock-

that some say the name of Penwith is derived from *pen-gwaed*, the bloody headland.

The other contestants for Cornish tin were the Jewish slaves which the Romans were supposed to have used in the mines. Some of them must have become freemen and exploited the mines themselves, for the chief harbour from which it was exported was Marazion, or Market Jew. In the last four hundred years or so, the tinners would tell of old workings haunted by knockers, buccas and spriggins, the underground spirits who were said to be the ghosts of the Jews who crucified Christ.

Other supernatural beings are not so closely connected with the tin trade. This is a country of mermaids, ghosts and giants, and many of the strange rock formations have been ascribed to the whims of the latter. Sometimes they are described as tyrannical Norman lords changed into granite; or to have come into their present position because giants' wives, who carried such boulders in their apron pockets, flung them at anybody who earned their disapproval.

Even without bad-tempered giantesses, the land of Penwith is still not always immediately welcoming. Frequently covered by mist, it can put a cold, bleak cover over a summer's day; but when that mist lifts, I defy you to find any landscape more lyrical than the enclosed dells which form pockets in the southern part of the moor. Yet it is the constant nearness of the sea, pounding a rocky shore on three sides of you, that gives the place its particular power. Symons even found that the hotel at Land's End, and the coming and going of many people, could not disturb the 'essential solitude' of this 'remote, rocky and barren land'. And although the traffic has increased so much since his time, the rocky coast and the inland moor, so continually washed by sea, winds and cloud, are free from the sterile exhaustion that kills most much frequented places.

Indeed, today's visitors are still overshadowed by the potent relics of the men who worked in the mines in historic times, and by those far more distant tinners and farmers who built the settlements at Carn Euny and Chysauster, as well as by the even earlier peoples who left riddling traces of their religious and social customs in the stone circles and menhirs of the moor.

Because it is so rich in folklore and history, the comparatively small geographical area of Penwith stretches through vast aeons of time, and the walks in this section thread millennia. The first, which is the logical conclusion of any journey through the Southwest, follows the last section of the dragon path to Land's End. It goes to a shore in which the commercialism of the tourist trade, with its seaside chalets, caravan parks and hotels, never really obscures the ancient mysteries. Still, it would be good if the promontory of Land's End itself were to be in the hands of some conservation body like the National Trust, instead of being left, as it is now, to the developing greed of the highest bidder. But at least the rocks and the waves that beat against them remain untouched by tourism; looking out to sea from here, the fabled country of Lyonnesse, which according to some traditions once lay between here and the Scilly Isles, seems to be much more valid than the ugly but relatively ephemeral buildings which exist to make money out of the visitors.

The second of the Penwith walks looks at other ley alignments in the area, drawing mainly on those discovered by John Michell (*Old Stones of Land's End*, 1979); the third returns to the vision of Richard Long, who made a walk through the interior of the moor from one prehistoric site to another; and the last traces the trading routes of the tinners as they went across the peninsula from the far northwest to Mount's Bay, by way of the Hayle estuary.

Walk 12
The Dragon Path to Land's End

From Bodmin Moor the dragon path runs through the length of Cornwall to the village of Sancreed [203: 420294], west of Penzance. This walk starts from Sancreed church along a footpath that runs just south of the dragon line but roughly parallel to it as it goes past Boswarthen [203: 413289] to the ancient and mysterious settlement of Carn Euny [203: 402289]. The whole of this area bears dramatic evidence of having been heavily populated for millennia, and its mystery lies in the way the successions of different peoples have influenced one another.

Across the lane from the tiny settlement of Brane [203: 403284] there is a Neolithic long barrow, which was used as a sheep shelter for at least two hundred years before it became an established and preserved ancient monument. It is no doubt that such use helped to keep its central passage

and kerbed mound intact, whatever one may feel about the desecration of a once sacred site. Probably the people who were buried here came from a settlement on or near the present Carn Euny to the north, although most of the outlines of buildings to be seen there now date from the Iron Age.

The banks along the lanes around Brane and Carn Euny are covered with shining leaves and white flowers of a giant penny royal, which flourishes throughout Cornwall. They make a pleasant approach to the prehistoric settlement, the remains of whose courtyard houses were first discovered by miners prospecting for tin in the middle of the last century. These houses were probably built around 500 BC and occupied throughout the Roman period. The most dramatic structure in the settlement, however, is believed to be of a much earlier date. Indeed it could even be

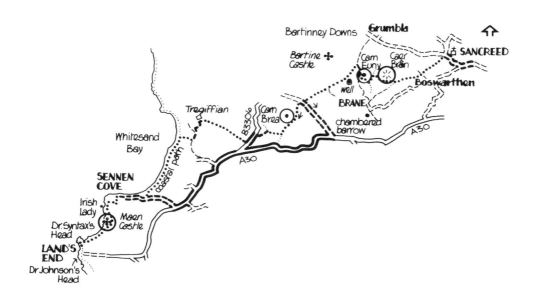

Fogou at Carn Euny

contemporary with the long barrow, for a Stone Age axe, quern and several flint implements have been found here. Perhaps it was the original owners of those things who were responsible for the building of this 'fogou', a semi-underground structure of drystone walling roofed with large granite slabs. This sort of underground building, used neither for burial nor (as far as anybody has been able to prove) for grain storage, is peculiar to Cornwall, although it has some resemblance to the sous-terrains of Brittany. The Cornish fogous all differ slightly from one another. The one at Carn Euny has a round chamber to the west

of it, connected by a trench to the main tunnel.

It is impossible to know what sort of ceremonies went on here, though it is tempting to think that they may have had some connection with the present name of the settlement, for Uny was an Etruscan earth goddess, who seems more appropriate to the place than St Euny, brother of St Ia of St Ives, who founded a church at Redruth. That preference is subjective, and so too is the feeling of spaciousness that I got in this damp building, which is in fact rather cramped. Like Philip Larkin considering churches fallen out of use, I found this 'a serious place'.

Above the settlement is the hill fort of Caer Brân [203: 407290], whose fortifications and causewayed entrance to the northwest can still be easily traced. It must have afforded protection to the farmers and tin streamers at Goldherring and Bartinney Hill as well as at Carn Euny itself. It could have been that security which gave Caer Brân its present local reputation as a sanctuary from evil spirits.

Another power for good in the area is the well of St Euny, which is to be found just by the track that runs southwest from the lane to Grumbla. Seven steps lead down to this spring, which is surrounded by stones that were probably once part of a chapel. Children brought here on the first three Wednesdays in May could be cured of their ailments.

From here the footpath goes south of Bartinney Down towards the hill of Carn Brea [203: 385280], where all the centuries come together. For on these heights, from which it is possible to glimpse the Scilly Isles, is a clump of barrows. On top of the largest of these, which was once a Neolithic tomb of some splendour, a chapel was built in AD 1300 and dedicated to St Michael. It was connected with the priory at St Michael's Mount, which decreed that a hermit should live on this western hill and keep a beacon alight to guide travellers by land and sea. After the Reformation the chapel fell into ruins; it was completely destroyed in 1816. But that is not the end of the story, for on 15 May 1971 the whole hill was given to the National Trust as a result of the pilgrimages of Margaret Keturah Fulleylove Thornley. It was acquired as a memorial to this remarkable woman by a group of her friends and admirers, who thought it fitting that she should be remembered at the site of a St Michael chapel.

Carn Brea

Dr Syntax Head

Margaret Thornley died in the early 1960s, after a lifetime spent in the continual awareness of the guardianship of the Archangel Michael, who vanquishes the powers of darkness. When she was made a Bard of the Cornish Gorsedd on Trencrom Hill, she chose the name Maghteth Myghal (handmaid of Michael); and between 1947 and 1956 she dedicated much of her time to making pilgrimages to the St Michael sites throughout Britain and Europe.

From Carn Brae you can either go downhill to rejoin the dragon path where it crosses the A30 and then follow the main road until it reaches the lane going down to Sennen Cove, or you can join the coastal path and take the slightly longer way to Land's End. To do that, follow the farm track to the B3306, and then take the bridlepath past Tregiffian [203: 367279]. South from here the coastal path runs above Whitesand Bay, a stretch of sandy beach which is ideal for swimming and surf riding, but which can be very dangerous in certain combinations of wind and tide. So look out for the warning signals.

Round Sennen Cove the sands give way to great rock formations which look like some giant exhibition of sculpture. Here in stone is an Irish lady looking out to sea, her cloak wrapped around her. She is just one of many impressive shapes slowly carved out by the waves. It was among these rocks that the ill-fated Perkin Warbeck made his stealthy landing in 1497 to start his unsuccessful bid for the throne of England. Obviously he was not the first invader to try it, for a little way back from the sea's surge is the Iron Age fort of Maen Castle [203: 348258]. It used the steep cliffs to the west as its main defence, and its entrance lay to the east. This earthwork needs some patience to interpret, but you can still see the two stones that mark that entrance, although only one is standing. Archaeologists have proved that, despite traces of agriculture by the eastern entrance, this fort was constructed for serious defensive purposes. The ditch outside the rampart was originally 9 feet deep, and the inner edge was pounded so smooth that it must have been impossible to climb. There is no evidence of any settlement inside the fort, unless you count the legend that it was the home of a giant whose child was stolen by the giant who lived across the moor at Showjack Farm.

From Maen Castle the coastal path runs over Peal headland, where it passes the rock whose profile has earned it the name of Dr Syntax's Head and which is the most westerly point of Britain. The coastal path continues south to the acknowledged Land's End, which is no longer any place to linger in during the holiday season, and round to the rocks of Dr Syntax's companion, Dr Johnson's Head, where the dragon path finally runs into the sea. This place marks the limit of one of Britain's oldest trackways, which stretched east through Avebury, and then, as the Icknield Way, linked the centre of England to the sea off the Norfolk coast. It was this westerly end of it, however, that linked Britain to the rest of the world, as the Bronze Age traders came looking for tin.

Now the Longships lighthouse is moored off these rocks, and swooping black-backed gulls which nest to the south of Enys Dodnan fly over the waves that separate the mainland from the Isles of Scilly, 28 miles away to the southwest. The souls of the dead were supposed to make that journey across the sea to the Isles of the Blessed, harried all the time they made the crossing by a great black dog. In the sixteenth century the legend changed. Then romance had it that these waves covered the sunken land of Lyonnesse, which, as John Norden tells, was 'swallowed up by the devouring sea'. Only one person is supposed to have escaped that flood, and he did so by riding to shore on a white horse.

Walk 13

Boscawen-noon to the Mên-an-tol

The second walk through the Land's End peninsula follows an extended course of some of the alignments noted by John Michell in *The Old Stones of Land's End* (1979). The first two pivot on the stone circle of Boscawen-noon, one approaching it from St Clement's Isle by Mousehole to the southeast, and the other going away from it to the northeast by the standing stone of the Blind Fiddler to the hill fort of Castle-an-Dinas. The third goes due west, from that stronghold to the famous holed stone, the Mên-an-tol.

The walk starts opposite St Clement's Isle, in the little harbour of Mousehole [203: 472255], which is one of the most picturesque villages in Cornwall and likely to be very crowded in high summer. It is a fitting place to start a pilgrimage, for although this walk goes inland to a holy site of the Bronze Age, it was from Mousehole, once a much more important harbour than Penzance, that English pilgrims of the Middle Ages started on their journeys to Rome and the Holy Land.

The strange name of the village has nothing to do with mice. It comes from a combination of *maew*, meaning a gull, and *holl*, a coombe; and it is right that it should be associated with sea-birds, for it houses a wild bird sanctuary and hospital where creatures injured through men's greed and carelessness are given shelter until they can be restored to their natural life. Visitors are welcomed to walk through the garden where the bird patients are nursed in high netted enclosures and see for themselves the misery caused by oil pollution. It is a far worse suffering than the two Yglesais sisters could have imagined when they founded their hospital in 1928.

The bird sanctuary stands to the right of the lane going uphill out of the town past the Methodist chapel. If you visit it, leave by the gate at the top of the garden, turn right along the lane and

then take the footpath across the fields to Trevithal [203: 464255]. From there the walk goes to the farm of Rose Vale [203: 447258] by Kerris, an area which is more fully explored in the course of Walk 14.

Sadly the footpath going west from Kerris Farm has now fallen out of use, and there is no direct way to follow the alignment over Bojewans Carn

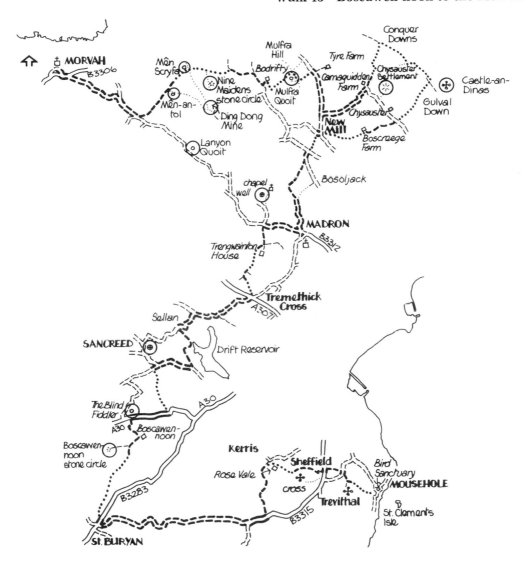

to the stone circle. The farm track going south from Rose Vale crosses the alignment, and from that point it is necessary to make for the lane going to St Buryan [203: 409257] and approach the circle from that village.

Here, where Athelstan founded his church in 932 in thanks offering for his successful mission to the Scilly Isles, another stone circle once stood.

Inside the present church, whose tall tower is a landmark for miles around, are two relics of the pagan worshippers at this place: a flint knife and a Bronze Age battle axe.

The way to the circle, which is still standing, goes up towards the farm of Boscawen-noon [203: 419276] just to the north of the alignment. From there the stones are approached by a narrow

Stone circle
Boscowan Moor

green lane running between high banks. This is usually a very muddy walk, but the circle itself well repays the scramble. It lies in a small enclosed dell, filled in spring and early summer with brilliant bluebells and wild violets. Yet even without the flowers it remains one of the most beautiful, if not the most dramatic of Britain's stone circles.

According to the medieval Welsh *Triads*, it was one of the three places where Gorsedds of Celtic poetry were held; the other two were at Old Sarum and Bryn Gwyddon. In 1928 when the Gorsedd was revived, it was held here among the eighteen granite stones that make up this circle. I hope that proper use was made then of the nineteenth, opposite the entrance, which is composed of white quartz, and which was obviously of great significance to the original circle builders.

In the middle of the last century, somebody erected an enclosing stone wall, now almost completely overgrown with thorns and brambles. This obscures the numbers of outlying stones aligned on the circle, but their positions have caused John Michell to consider that this site was the most important Megalithic complex southwest of Stonehenge. According to Michell, Sir Norman Lockyer, the nineteenth-century astro-archaeologist, was of the same opinion when he came to work out its orientations to the May and November sunrises. According to one derivation its name comes from *bos* (flash) and *ca ombain* (the dawn), but neatly as this fits in with Lockyer's observations, the more probable derivation is from *bos scawen an wun* (the settlement by the elder tree on the downs).

John Barnatt, who has made a close study of the stone circles of both Derbyshire and Cornwall, points out that this 'circle', unlike most of those in Cornwall, is not a true circle and that it never could have been wherever the three re-erected stones were placed. He imagines that Boscawen-noon must have been originally designed as some sort of ellipse with square corners.

The alignment, which goes northeast from this circle, passes through the Blind Fiddler [203: 416282], a long thin slab of granite studded with quartz which stands almost 11 feet high. The Tresvennack Pillar and the stones of Drift, which are visited during Walk 14, are both visible from it. From Boscawen-noon's great outrider the walk goes along the bridlepath to Sancreed, whose ruined chapel with St Credan's holy well [203: 420295] beneath it has much more to offer than the restored parish church.

The way to the cleared site where the chapel once stood, a field to the north of the church, has been fully described by Gerald Priestland in *West of Hayle River*. The well, which was rediscovered by the vicar in 1879, is a model of the best sort of Victorian preservation; it is approached by a flight of rough steps.

The walk goes on along the lane running southeast from the village and then goes north round the Drift Reservoir *via* Sellan and the lane to Tremethick Cross [203: 445305]. From there footpaths go past Trengwainton House to Madron, with its restored thirteenth-century church. Once again the well [203: 445327] with its attendant chapel, which in this case stands about a mile to the north of the village, is by far the more interesting site. It is one of the many healing wells of Cornwall in which children were dipped to cure them of rickets. The ritual had to be performed on the first three Sunday mornings in May, and to make sure the cure was effective, the parents had

to keep silent and face the sun as their children were plunged three times into the water. If the water bubbled when the child was being dipped, or if the youngster went to sleep after the immersion, it was a sign that the cure was effective.

Today the 'well' is simply a spring in the middle of a pool whose waters have overflowed down the path, which is now so excessively muddy as to be virtually impassable without waders. The baptistry in which its waters were also employed is much more easily reached. This beautiful ruin, with stone benches round three of its inner walls, is roofless now; but the stone altar still stands by the

Baptistry, Madron

Chysauster

O Caldecott

fourth wall, and a stream runs into a basin in the southwest corner. In the small enclosure outside the chapel there is a hawthorn tree to which people still attach rags, which are supposed to carry on their owners' supplications as they flap in the wind. All around the dell in which it stands bluebells, celandine and white wild garlic grow. On my last visit, I was fortunate enough to have a goldfinch complete the enchantment.

From Madron the way goes north of the alignment past Bosoljack [203: 455329] to New Mill [203: 458341], and from there by the footpath by Boscreege Farm [203: 468341] to the lane for Chysauster [203: 473350], whose Iron Age hill village is now in the care of the Department of the Environment. This settlement stands on the alignment from Castle-an-Dinas to the Mên-an-tol, but is now fenced round in such a way that it is only possible to approach it legally from the lane.

It is lucky for us that this truly remarkable village has been so well preserved. In 1899 Baring-Gould found that the tenant farmer had begun to destroy one of the huts, and he rightly and modestly observed that 'They ought to be investigated by such as are experienced and trained in excavation of such objects, and not be meddled with by amateurs.' I feel that the present preservation would have pleased him, for he was well aware of the value of this site. 'There are other collections of a similar character,' he wrote, 'but none so perfect.'

The early farmers and tin miners who set up this village before the Romans came, and whose descendants went on living here until the third century AD, chose a beautiful site on the western slopes of the hill. Their circular houses, with their small terraced gardens, are set in pairs on either side of a main street. Each one consists of a courtyard surrounded by a series of rooms encased by the enclosing wall. On the hill below the remains of the houses is the fogou, reduced to a humped mound with a cave-like entrance.

The way to the Celtic fort of Castle-an-Dinas

Walk 13 Boscawen-noon to the Mên-an-tol

[203: 484351], which stands above Chysauster, climbs over Gulval Downs by a path which leaves the lane beside the farm to the south of the settlement. This hill fort dates from the second or third century BC, and from the top of the hill on which it stands you can see the great fort of Trencrom to the east, which is visited on Walk 15.

Entrance to fogou

Fogou, looking out

The traces of the huts which once sheltered within the ramparts of Castle-an-Dinas, have not been so well treated by posterity as those of the village on the hillside below them. In 1798 many of them were destroyed to make room for the folly of Roger's Tower. The builders of that tower may also have obliterated the traces of the well that Dr Borlase noted some forty years earlier for there are no signs of it now. But apparently they did nothing to disturb the ghost of Wild Harris, condemned by Parson Pilkinghorne to make nine counts of every blade of grass within the inner enclosure and to reach the same total each time before he could be at peace.

Castle-an-Dinas is the start of a new alignment to the west which goes straight downhill to the Chysauster settlement. But as there is no proper public path that way now, the walker must follow the main track, which can be exceptionally wet and muddy. It joins the farm way that goes downhill to Carnaquidden Farm [203: 468350], a

building that also stands on the alignment. From here the lane goes steeply downhill to a T junction. Turn right and go north for about a mile until you come to the bridge leading to Trye Farm. On the opposite side of the lane you will see a narrow footpath leading steeply uphill to Mulfra Quoit [203: 452354]. It stands high up on the hillside in a clearing in the heather. The great capstone has slipped off its three supports, but it is still an impressive sight, and it obviously served as a landmark for many of the settlements around. From Chysauster it stands out on the horizon to the west, and from the circle of the Nine Maidens, the next point on this walk, it is visible to the east.

The hut settlement by the quoit actually lies on the Castle-an-Dinas/Mên-an-tol alignment which runs just south of the Nine Maidens [203: 434353], whose two tallest stones frame the great rock stack above Morvah. Another rather swampy track from the Nine Maidens circle goes past disused mine shafts to Ding Dong Mine, which forms part of Walk 15 (see page 124). Now the walk goes northwest from the circle to the Mên Scryfa, or inscribed stone, which stands alone in a field at the top of a hill, above a small dell with a ruined cottage in it. The stone is engraved 'Rialobrani'; the name means royal raven, and he has been equated with the giant Holiburn. The inscription is thought to date from the fifth or sixth century AD, but the stone itself, which measures nearly 10 feet, was put on this site in the Neolithic era and, as John Michell has shown, it stands on the alignment running from the Nine Maidens circle to Mulfra Quoit.

Until 1824, the Mên Scryfa had lain for centuries on its side, supposedly tipped up by a speculator who had heard that a crock of gold might be found buried here. From this place a much used bridlepath, which has been deeply cut into the slope of the moor, runs downhill past the footpath to the Mên-an-tol [203: 427344], the holed stone, which marks the final point on this alignment. This famous stone stands midway between two upright ones, with a space of approximately 8 feet between each stone. No one yet knows how this strange little monument came to be here, or how the hole in the Mên-an-tol was

Men-an-Tol

Lanyon Quoit

formed; it is even doubtful whether any of the stones are in their original positions. In fact the most certain thing about the group is the superstition that adhered to it. Up to the early years of this century, it was common practice to pass naked children through the Mên-an-tol, seeing to it that each movement through the stone is made with the child's back to the sun, to cure them of rickets and other childhood diseases. Dr Borlase, who visited the site in 1749, had no hesitation in putting the practice down to a druidic initiation rite, a hypothesis favoured by his contemporary antiquarians.

From the Mên-an-tol you can either break into Walk 15 by continuing southeast along the path going to the Ding Dong Mine [203: 435347], or return to the bridlepath and continue downhill until you join the lane that goes northwest to Morvah and southeast to Lanyon Quoit [203: 430337].

Because it stands by the roadside, this quoit, which was knocked down by a storm in 1815 and

rebuilt to its present shape nine years later, is the best known of Penwith's prehistoric monuments. Going north from here, the lane which leads to Morvah [203: 402355] was once the main route taken by people travelling to the village's Lammas Fair which marked the beginning of harvest. This festival is now celebrated by the church on the first Sunday of August.

The fourteenth-century church, which was built by the Knights of St John, stands on the site of a Celtic settlement and chapel; but the St Bridget to whom it is dedicated is not the Celtic Bride, but St Bridget of Sweden, who founded a widespread religious order, and whose Brigittine nuns had a cell at St Michael's Mount in the fifteenth century. The present church was mostly rebuilt in the nineteenth, after the original building had become a ruin. A cow once chewed the frayed rope from the crumbling belfry, so setting off an eerie ringing of bells which only the miners were brave enough to investigate.

Walk 14
Richard Long's Walk

1978 a day's walk past the
standing stones of Penwith Peninsula
   The Pipers
   Kerris
   Tresvennack
   Drift
   The Blind Fiddler
   Boscawen-un
   Boswens
   Beersheba

This list was included in an exhibition of Richard Long's work held in the Museum of Modern Art in Oxford during 1979. There is no indication as to what paths this photographer/sculptor took as he traced this pattern on the landscape, so I have drawn a route between these landmarks which makes use of the best footpaths. In certain places I have extended the walk to enable us to visit other sites standing close to the ones he listed.

This walk does not begin at The Pipers where Richard Long's started but a little farther west along the B3315. Here we will find a way into the field where the nineteen 4-foot-high stones of the Merry Maidens circle [203: 435246] are to be found. The original local name for this circle was Dawn Maen, or dancing stones, but as with other circles in this country which share similar names, it was the maidens (or rather the witches who used them as a meeting place) who actually did the

The Merry Maidens

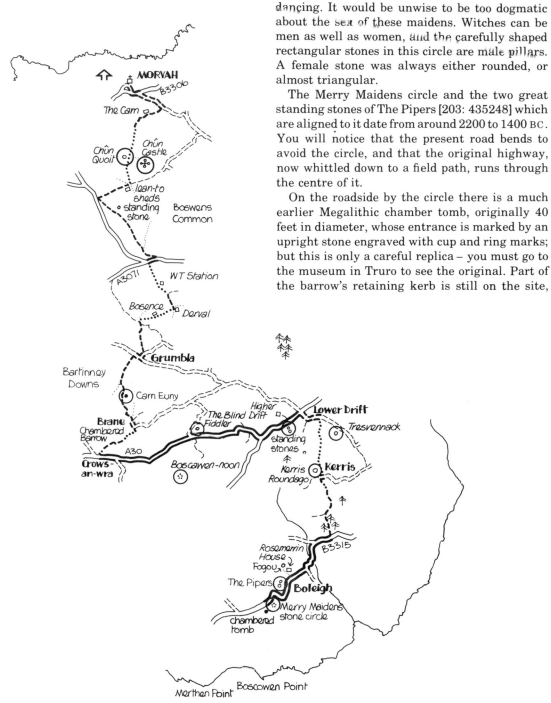

dancing. It would be unwise to be too dogmatic about the sex of these maidens. Witches can be men as well as women, and the carefully shaped rectangular stones in this circle are male pillars. A female stone was always either rounded, or almost triangular.

The Merry Maidens circle and the two great standing stones of The Pipers [203: 435248] which are aligned to it date from around 2200 to 1400 BC. You will notice that the present road bends to avoid the circle, and that the original highway, now whittled down to a field path, runs through the centre of it.

On the roadside by the circle there is a much earlier Megalithic chamber tomb, originally 40 feet in diameter, whose entrance is marked by an upright stone engraved with cup and ring marks; but this is only a careful replica – you must go to the museum in Truro to see the original. Part of the barrow's retaining kerb is still on the site,

Two Pipers

however; it is all that has survived the ravages of time and road builders.

From here the walk goes east along the road towards the village of Boleigh, where tradition has it that the Saxon, Athelstan, fought a fierce battle against Howel and his Cornish forces in 936. The name Boleigh or Bolleit certainly means the place of slaughter or house of blood, but whether it commemorates that or an earlier battle I cannot say, although one legend has it that The Pipers represent Athelstan and Howel. These two outriders of the Merry Maidens circle are now separated by a field hedge, and stand just north of the road and to the west of the village. They are among the tallest stones in Cornwall, being 15 feet and 13½ feet respectively, yet surprisingly they are invisible from the circle itself. Usually known as The Pipers, they are also sometimes spoken of locally as the Giant's Grave, and taken to mark the head and foot of some enormous burial.

As well as being linked to the Merry Maidens, the two stones stand on individual ley alignments of their own, and these have been noted by John Wilcock in his *Guide to Occult Britain* (Sphere, 1977). The tallest one, which stands to the north-east, is on a line that is linked to the Mousehole–Boscawen-noon alignment; the other, which stands higher up on the ridge, is aligned to the standing stone to the north of Kerris, to which this walk is now heading.

John Barnatt, who is both a professional artist and an archaeologist, has given a lot of time to the orientation of standing stones throughout Britain; he reckons that the sheer weight of The Pipers would require at least forty people to have a hand in erecting them. He argues from the magnitude of that undertaking that it would be quite absurd to suggest that they are randomly sited.

We start off on Richard Long's walk by going about a mile northeast along the road; this will take us to the fogou which stands near the banks of the Lamorna river in the grounds of Rosemerrin House [203: 436243]. This underground structure is on the alignment to Kerris, and goes through the farther Piper to the coast between Merthen and Boscawen Points.

Walk 14   Richard Long's Walk

Jo May, who lives at Rosemerrin, welcomes visitors to come and look at the fogou and is happy to answer questions about it. He explains how the temperature inside the cave will rise in the same way as it does in one of the 'orgone chambers', enclosures built up of alternate layers of organic and inorganic matter, devised by the psychologist Wilhelm Reich. Jo also explains why he believes that the fogou was used for both good and evil. It was from him that I learned the horrific story of the use to which the circular side chamber is said to have been put. It stands to the west of the main gallery and is reached by a creep passage from it. They say that pregnant girls were walled in here until they had given birth to the child, who was to be the victim of magic rites. To counteract that horror, however, Mr May will show you the carving on one of the entrance stones. It is of a human figure holding a spear and snake aloft, and it is thought to represent the Celtic god of healing.

The place was used as a refuge by Royalists at the time of the Civil War, and they were no doubt content to forget the strange reputation of the underground gallery which gave them shelter in extremity. But the stories went on, telling how witches (perhaps the very ones who also danced at the Merry Maidens) were supposed to hold their sabbats here, and how when they were surprised they changed into hares and hid in the far chamber.

Across the river, a farm track leads due north for Kerris. Kerris Roundago [203: 442274] stands behind a former chapel which has now been converted into a private house. It was originally a large, oval enclosure, but much of it has been ploughed up now, and only the two great uprights of the entrance make it known to the uninitiated that this was ever a place of some importance. Most of the wall which once surrounded this settlement was dismantled in 1840 to build the breakwater at Penzance; but when Halliwell took his rambles in western Cornwall in 1861, he was told that the walls were wide enough for a cart to be driven along the top. No one knows the exact purpose of the original building, but it was locally regarded as a sacred place, so nobody was much surprised when its desecration was marked by the death of the horses which were used to remove the stones.

The term 'round' in the Southwest usually refers to small Iron Age settlements, and this may also explain the Kerris enclosure, but the two stones that stand to the north of it are certainly of a much earlier date. The first, only 200 yards away, is thought to belong to the Bronze Age. It is a triangular slab of stone of the shape usually taken to represent female power, or to denote the burial place of an important woman. The second is the great male pillar of Tresvennack [203: 442268], which stands over 11 feet tall, and which marks one point on a northwestern alignment from the Boscawen-noon circle. John Michell reports in *The Old Stones of Land's End* (1979) that, in 1840, a farmer digging round the foot of this pillar discovered an 18-inch square slab of stone beneath which were two urns, one of which contained cremated bones. These urns are now in the Penzance museum, and confirm that this pillar also belongs to the Bronze Age.

From the farm beyond it, a grassy lane runs towards the next point on Richard Long's walk, the standing stones of Drift [203: 436273]. These two stones stand on high ground in a field just opposite the lane to Higher Drift Farm. They are 9 feet and 7 feet tall respectively, and stand some 18 feet apart. When W. C. Borlase excavated them in 1871, he discovered that a carefully cut pit, measuring 6 feet by 3 feet 3 inches, lay between them, and naturally described this as a grave, although it contained no evidence of any human remains.

From these stones you can see both the Tresvennack Pillar and the Blind Fiddler, which is the next standing stone on the list. It can only be reached by travelling west along the A30. Walk 13 goes past that stone and the Boscawen-noon circle (see page 104), which Richard Long made the next points on his itinerary, but which are not included in this walk.

The new part of the walk for us starts some 3 miles west along the A30 at the village of Crows-an-wra [203: 395277], whose name means the witch's cross. The cross is wheel-headed and stands beside an ornate milestone in the centre of

The Blind Fiddler

the village. The witch has been identified as Harry the Hermit, who once lived in the chapel that stood on top of the great barrow of Carn Brea (see page 99).

From the village the walk goes northeast along the footpath which passes the Neolithic chambered barrow at Brane (see page 97) and north along the track to the west of the Iron Age village of Carn Euny [203: 402289]. From there it goes along the sandy bridlepath that runs below Bartinney Downs to Grumbla [203: 404298], and so north past Bosence [203: 407305] and Derval [203: 413306] to the wireless station by the A3071. The track from that road runs down the west side of Boswens Common past the last marker on Richard Long's list in this region.

This stone [203: 400328] stands a little way to the east of the path on open moorland, and it can

Standing stone, near Chûn Quoit

be seen for miles around. It is a pillar of lichen-covered granite in the form of a kneeling straight-backed figure, and must have served as an observation post as well as a landmark, for its most remarkable feature are two rough steps cut in its western side, which John Michell considers were deliberately made so that the pillar could be climbed.

Richard Long gave Beersheba, by Trencrom Hill Fort, as the last point on his itinerary, but this is so far to the east that I am leaving it to Walk 15, and ending this one with a visit to Chûn Castle [203: 405339]. To get there continue north to the sandy track which runs east along the valley, and follow it as far as some corrugated lean-to sheds and an old brown caravan. From that point the Longstone on Boswens Common and the mass of Chûn Quoit [203: 402340] are both visible on the skyline.

Chûn Quoit is reached by a heather-covered track that climbs the hill to the north. As you go along it you will find that you lose the quoit for a while, but if you turn round as soon as it comes into view again, you will find that you can also see the Longstone behind you. The quoit has four upright stones which form a closed chamber and a massive capstone, making it one of the grandest of the Cornish quoits. Along the ridge to the east of the small mound on which it stands are the stones of Chûn Castle, whose great western entrance faces Chûn Quoit and the Kenidjack cairn, which is one of the places visited on Walk 15.

Chûn Quoit

Chûn Castle.

This 'castle' was once a massive fortification, being built entirely of stone during the third century BC, and it is still amazingly impressive. It was here that the tin of Penwith was brought for storage and smelting before being taken along routes, which are covered in Walk 15, to the ports on the Hayle estuary and at St Michael's Mount.

Legend has it that Chûn Castle was built by Jack the Tinner, who had all the cunning of his craft, for he was taken as being the original Jack the Giant Killer. But modestly enough, he and his wife, Jennifer, are supposed to have made their home beneath the capstone of the quoit, which pre-dates the castle by some three thousand years.

Walk 15

The Tinners' Road to St Michael's Mount

There are two main tinners' routes across the Cornish peninsula. The one which went across Bodmin Moor from Tintagel to Fowey was described in Part Two. The western route goes from the Hayle estuary to St Michael's Mount. This walk, which follows that way, goes by the mines and tin workings at the very west of Penwith, and then takes the road to St Ives, making a very slight detour to the east. The first part of this walk follows a coastline known to the Greek Pytheas, who in the latter part of the fourth century BC sailed through the Strait of Gibraltar to Land's End, where he made friends with the Cornish tin streamers before starting to circumnavigate Britain.

If Pytheas had come back to this peninsula at any time during the next two thousand years he would have found the countryside much as he left it, for this part of Penwith from St Just to St Ives remained without roads until the end of the eighteenth century. None are noted in the road survey undertaken in 1748; even as late as 1637 there were still no carts in the county, so that everything had to be carried by horses, which were laden, as they were in Pytheas's time, with panniers or heavy yokes, known as crooks, on which pots or baskets were suspended. The only great change that would have struck him would have been the wayside crosses, the great spires of some of the churches and a few of the farm buildings, although if he had come back during the Middle Ages, he would have found that several of the old Celtic settlements had simply been enlarged and adapted.

Later, of course, he would have found, as we do, that the mine chimneys dominated the coastline. Yet the first part of this walk goes past a place which he must have been shown and of which the very early tinners were afraid. The walk starts

Ballowall Barrow & tin mine

just to the south of St Just aerodrome [203: 377288] and goes across Travegean Downs to join the coastal path by Gribba Point [203: 355302], where it heads north for Cape Cornwall, passing by the great, stony, Neolithic mound of Ballowall Barrow [203: 355313] whose roofless dome stands 10 feet above the disused mine shafts of Carn Gluze. Long after Pytheas's time, the tinners, returning from their work at night, used to say that they saw lights burning and fairies dancing round the walls of this most unusual barrow, and it is indeed an eerie place even in broad daylight. A feeling of doom hangs over it, and this is now increased by the warnings about uncovered mine shafts on each side of the path. This is no place to visit in a mist, when the mound of the barrow looms up in an unearthly way, and the pits in the actual earth could be anywhere beneath your feet.

If you come here on a clear day that is right for exploring and investigating, you will find a double barrow, the outer wall, in which a single wall burial was found, surrounding an inner dry stone vault, which was originally corbelled. Steps from the south side lead into this chamber, which contains an odd T-shaped pit, which is presumed to have had some ritual significance. From here the path continues north to the settlement at Cape

Cornwall [203: 350319], whose land has been farmed since the Bronze Age. The remains of the tin workings impinge most dramatically on this landscape. A mine chimney is perched on the very headland of Cape Cornwall, with the coastguard lookout station beneath it, and a ruined chapel standing in the middle of a ploughed field just behind it. From now on the walker can never forget the mines.

This is the landscape remembered in W. S. Graham's lament for the painter, Peter Lanyon, killed in a gliding accident in 1964, and one to challenge the vision of any poet or artist:

'Shall we go down' you said
'Before the light goes
And stand under the old
Tinworkings around
Morvah and St Just?'
You said 'Here is the sea
Made by alfred wallis
Or any poet or painter's
Eye it encountered
Or is it better made
By all those vesselled men
Sometime it maintained?
We all make it again.'

Ballowall Barrow

121

Coastline, Cape Cornwall

So every walker will interpret his own landscape out of the dramatic ingredients of wave, pinnacled cliffs, mine chimneys and barrows as he walks from Cape Cornwall past the headland of Kenidjack Castle [203: 354326] to Boscaswell. This whole area is thick with mine workings, some of which extend under the sea beneath Botallack Head. When Celia Fiennes rode this way in the seventeenth century, she found that twenty tin mines could be seen at one time, and that more than a thousand men were working in them.

These mines continued in use into this century, and romantic as the old workings look now, the reality on which they were built was dreadful. In the 1920s, the men who worked here, and who lived in the back-to-back cottages along the St Just road to Cape Cornwall, earned little more than £2 a week; but they were better off than their nineteenth-century predecessors whose working life began at the age of twelve, and who had an average life expectancy of twenty-five years. During that time they were in the mines on ten-hour shifts.

Now, after decades of idleness, the mines are starting up again, for tin is being realized as a valuable commodity once more. In Pendeen the Geevor tin mines have their own museum, and visitors can go underground to see part of the plant in action. The less adventurous can go to the centre of the village, where one of the craft shops has mounted a display showing the history of the mines through the centuries.

The best way to approach Pendeen from the coastal path is to go through Lower Boscaswell [203: 377348] to the lane which runs past Pendeen Manor Farm [203: 380356], where the eighteenth-century Cornish antiquarian William Borlase was born. It is sometimes possible to visit the fogou or *vau* which lies just behind this house, but application must first be made to the owner of Manor Farm. It is well worth doing so, for the steep entrance leading to this underground chamber is so impressive that tradition has it that it leads to a gallery which extends under the sea to the Scilly Isles.

From the village of Pendeen, the walk goes inland by the ruins of Wheal Bal [203: 384334], and over the eerie Gump to the rock stack on Cairn Kenidjack [203: 387329] which dominates the skyline for miles around, almost dwarfing the wireless telegraph mast beside it. This rock-strewn common is full of Bronze Age barrows and anyone walking there will understand why it has acquired the reputation of being a haunt of witches, and why they say that the devil rides on a half-starved horse through this wasteland, chasing after anyone who dares to come this way at night.

In daylight, the walker can safely follow the path by the series of boundary stones which lead up to the cairn. From that height you can look back the way you have come as far as St Just, and south to Carn Brea and Bartinney Downs, the hills which separate the northern from the southern part of Penwith. A fairly wide sandy track goes down to the road from here, the lane opposite the

Disused mines
Botallok

turning to the farm of Boslow [203: 395327] going past the barrow which is marked on the OS map as Carnworth Circles.

Across the main road below the Longstone on Boswens Common and the strange modern circular installation above it, the wide track, which forms part of Walk 14, runs east below Chûn Quoit to Great Bosullow [203: 415336]. Across the lane from that little cluster of houses a footpath over the moor goes to the ruined chimney of Ding Dong Mine. From there the walk goes past the Nine Maidens circle (see page 108), north towards the rocks of Carn Galver [203: 425365] and then east to Bosporthennis Farm [203: 438364] and the lane that leads to Porthmeor and Treen.

Craig Weatherhill's *Belerion*, a gazetteer of the ancient sites of Land's End, gives the derivation of the name Bosporthennis as 'dwelling at the entrance to an isolated spot', and although part of the high moorland here is divided into fields, the great windswept expanse is isolated enough. Yet it was not always so, for a large Iron Age settlement once stood at the southeastern end of Hannibal's Carn [203: 433364]. The most spectacular building to be found there now is a corbelled hut in the corner of a field. The walls of this beehive hut are over 7 feet high, but archaeologists do not think that it was ever a dwelling. It bears no resemblance to the structure of the general run of Celtic courtyard houses in Cornwall, and is in fact far more like the circular underground chamber attached to the Carn Euny fogou. For that reason it is thought to be some sort of surface fogou, and just as mysterious as the ones that run underground. A more typical courtyard dwelling, but one modified and preserved by its use in the Middle Ages, lies to the south of the beehive.

The lane from Bosporthennis to Treen [203: 436377] crosses the road which runs between Morvah and Zennor, and which is said to be haunted by Holiburn, the giant who lives among the rocks of Carn Galver hill. He is supposed to have died of grief seven years after he accidentally cracked a young man's skull, never realizing that human bone could be so fragile.

Just beside the Gurnard's Head Hotel at Treen a footpath goes to the coastal fort of Trereen Dinas

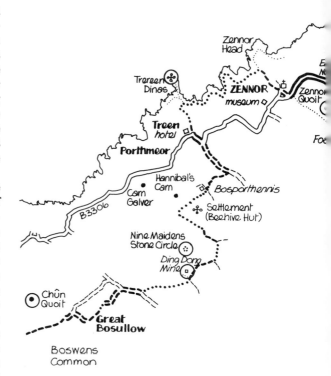

[203: 433387], whose lofty earthworks stand on a steep and narrow headland. The central entrance to the fort, and the only way it can be at all easily approached, is at the narrowest point of the headland. Although you can climb up to it now by the steps which have been put up at the east side of the rock face and which lead to the coast guard station, no attacker trying to scale the cliffs would stand any chance at all. The garrison which was forced to make its uncomfortable home here was needed to protect the route of the valuable tin trade, which was fought over as bitterly as, in economic terms, oil is today.

From this stronghold, the walk once more joins the coastal path, this time following it as far as Zennor Head [203: 449395], where it diverges into Zennor village, which has a little open air museum devoted to recording Cornish life and

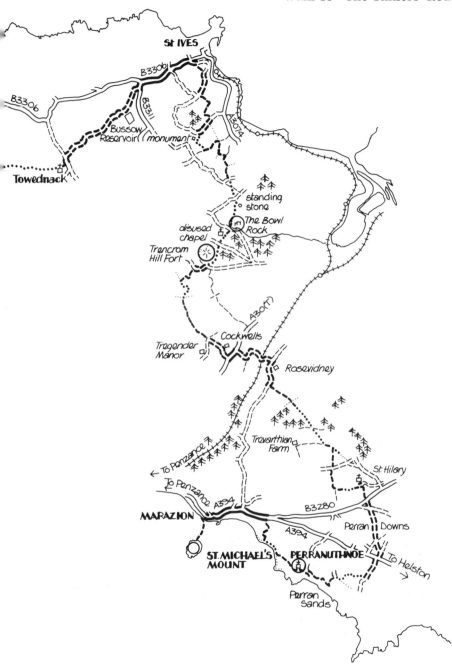

mining. In the south chapel of the church, Zennor's famous mermaid reclines. The story is that Sunday after Sunday a beautiful, unknown woman in a long dress appeared in church, for the purpose of listening to the voice of the chorister, Matthew Trewhella. One evening, it is said, she succeeded in luring him down to the water's edge, and neither of them was ever seen again. They say, however, that sometimes on a still, summer's night, you can hear Matthew and the mermaid singing beneath the waves.

The church is dedicated to St Senera who, like many another Celtic saint, established a holy place on her journey across Cornwall between Ireland and Brittany. Legend has identified her with the Breton Princess Asenora, whose stepmother, jealous of her beauty and virtue, accused her of being unfaithful to her husband, King Goello. She was condemned to be burned, but when her jailers found that she was pregnant, they feared to make themselves guilty of the outright murder of an unborn child. So they nailed her inside a barrel and threw it into the sea. In that state she was cared for by an angel who attended the birth of the child and fed her until the barrel was washed up on the Irish coast. Her son became Abbot of St Budoc and eventually returned with her to Brittany.

From Zennor the walk goes east, uphill along the road for about a quarter of a mile. It is along this stretch of road that the last fairy in England is said to have been captured. Perhaps he was a descendant of the pre-Celtic settlers whose ancestors founded one of the Bronze Age settlements on the moors in which he too took shelter from the aggressive tinners.

Opposite the large hilltop house, appropriately named Eagle's Nest, a white gate leads onto the moors and the path to a remote cottage. Just in front of the cottage is another path running between two walls, and this takes you to Zennor Quoit [203: 469380]. Like every other ruined stone tomb in the area – Chûn, Lanyon and Mulfra – this quoit is supposed to have been flung by giants into

Zennor Quoit

Trencrom Hill Fort

its present position. The particular superstition about this quoit, however, is that if its stones are ever removed they will return of their own accord to their original position. An attempt to try this out was supposed to have been made in 1861, and promptly stopped by the vicar, who luckily happened to be the Reverend William Borlase himself.

From this quoit the walk goes east to the church of St Twennocus at Towednack [203: 488383], a place whose peace must surely have exorcised any evil that was bred on the surrounding moor when, as they tell you, all the witches in Cornwall gathered on Trewey Downs on Midsummer Eve to renew their vows to the Devil as the solstice fires burned low.

St Ives, which is the next point on the walk, is still worth visiting for the Barbara Hepworth museum and sculpture garden, and for its network of steeply terraced narrow streets, but it is virtually simply little more than a tourist trap, and one you may soon want to leave in order to follow the tinners' way south to Marazion and St Michael's Mount. The start of that walk goes through the southern outskirts of the town, and leaves the streets to take to field paths [203: 525385] and a

Tremoran Hill Fort

flower-strewn green lane which leads into the next valley. The path goes by a standing stone [203: 525374] which I have heard called Beersheba, and which I have taken to be the final point on Richard Long's walk past the standing stones of Penwith. Perhaps it gets its name from the chapel below Trencrom Hill.

The path enters the valley by the great Bowl Rock [203: 523368], which has come to rest beside a stream whose banks are now beautifully tended by the owner of the nearby whitewashed cottage. Once again, this rock is supposed to have been giant-flung, this time from Trencrom Hill Fort. Other stones thrown from that place are meant to have been aimed at the spire of the church of St

Hilary and at St Michael's Mount. Both these places are on the tinners' routes, and I have discovered that legends of such giant-flung stones abound along ancient tracks.

Across the road from Bowl Rock you will see some steps in a wall. They lead to a path running beside a field of daffodils and past the disused chapel to the first slopes of Trencrom Hill. The Iron Age fort that crowns this bracken-covered hill has made use of the natural rock formations there. A single wall follows the contours of the hillside, with entrances to the east and west which still bear traces of the original paved causeway; inside are faint remains of seventeen of the huts which once stood on the flat ground at the summit.

When I went there last a herd of beautiful white goats was grazing on the site.

The southern slopes of this hill are much rockier than the northern side, so it can be quite a scramble to get down to the next lane and resume the walk across fields and moorland, lanes and old bridleways to the church of St Hilary [203: 550313], whose spire is visible from miles around. Indeed, as this church stands 190 feet above sea level it was able to serve as a landmark for ships coming into either the Hale Estuary or Mount's Bay. The site was a Christian place long before the tower and spire were built in the thirteenth century, although it remained unconsecrated until 1855 when much of the present church was built. That was not the end of the story, for in recent church history, St Hilary's is remembered as being the focal point of an attack by the militant low church Kensitites of the 1930s. These zealots forced their way into the building and took the sacred furnishings from the altar. That conflict seems to have given new life to the church, whose interior is now full of paintings by local artists and which houses a large crucifix made by Phyliss Yglesais, one of the sisters who founded the bird hospital at Mousehole.

From the church of St Hilary the tinners' route to Mount's Bay goes along sands which form the greatest possible contrast to the cliffs of the northwest. A little way inland is the church of St Piran at Perranuthnoe [203: 537295] which, according to John Michell's calculations, stands on a ley alignment to the circle at Boscawen-noon, going through the great pillar at Tresvennack. Perhaps that accounts for the double dedication of this church, for it is also given to St Michael the Archangel.

As for the Irish St Piran, he came to Cornwall at the end of the fifth century and built his famous oratory on the sands at Perranporth near Newquay. From there, like many another Irish saint, he crossed Cornwall on his way to Brittany. He was a very tall man, as can be judged from the height of the altar at Perranporth, and because of his strength and craft in devising a new method of smelting, he became a patron saint of the tinners. When he arrived at the site where Perranuthnoe stands now, the sea was a mile farther out than it is today. Under the waves there may well be another chapel founded by him and comparable to the one in the north, which lay hidden under sand dunes for a thousand years.

From the church at Perranuthnoe, a lane runs west above the allotments towards St Michael's Mount. Depending on the state of the tide, you can finish this walk by going along that lane to Marazion, or taking to the low rocks of this shore and going along by the sea. At very low tide you can walk to the Mount itself along the causeway built five hundred years ago with the money raised by penitents, who were granted forty days' remission of their penances if their contributions to the project were sufficiently large.

Like all rocky outcrops in Cornwall, the Mount is supposed to be the home of a giant. Its Christian history starts with a visit to this place by St Keyne and her nephew Caradoc in the sixth century. A hundred years later, after seeing a vision of St Michael himself, William of Worcester founded a monastery here, which was later supplanted by a Benedictine abbey. That was suppressed in 1425, and in 1497 the place gave shelter to the anxious wife of Perkin Warbeck, who left her here when he marched up country to Bodmin.

Now the rock is surmounted by an eighteenth-century house of great elegance, which is partly open to the public who come in their thousands throughout the summer. So once again, St Michael's Mount is as busy and cosmopolitan a commercial centre as it was when traders from distant lands bargained for the tin.

St Michael's Mount,
Cornwall

Walking on Granite

I have never seen a more dreary tract than that over which we passed from the tin mines towards Lidford. The soil is exceedingly swampy and moist, and covered with bog-moss (*Sphagnum palustre*) through which our horses' legs penetrated knee-deep at every step. If we had not been accompanied by the captain of the mines, who seemed to be well acquainted with the country, we should have been in unceasing apprehension of sinking deeper than our heads.

W. G. Maton, *Observations on the Western Counties of England*, 1794–6

Because water penetrates granite so slowly, walking on these moors presents two hazards: the bogs, encountered by the eighteenth-century traveller whose remarks on northwest Dartmoor are quoted above, and the rapidly descending and all-enveloping mists that can lead the unwary to walk into them. Bodmin Moor has bogs that are just as dangerous as those on Dartmoor, although they are much less extensive. There are safe, if not dry, routes through the quaking acres of the latter, but it is unwise to try them out without a competent guide.

The wide bogs make Dartmoor mists more dangerous than those of the other moors. A Dartmoor mist is like no other I have experienced. It seems to emerge out of an almost clear sky, advancing on every side until you are completely enclosed. William Crossing, who knew the moor as well as anybody could, declared in his *Guide to Dartmoor* that these mists are 'beyond map and compass because of bogs'. So he advised his readers to adopt the plan of following a stream 'as this will eventually run to one of the roads that confines the moor'. His advice is sound, so long as

you remember that on many stretches of Dartmoor's high and level valleys you may have to walk some distance before it becomes clear whether you are going up or down stream.

Crossing's advice is equally valid for Bodmin Moor, and for Penwith, where the streams heading for the sea lead you to the coastal road. The mists which envelop that moor come rolling in from the Atlantic with surprising speed and lift as rapidly as they come. They can saturate the unwary with penetrating cold even on a summer's day.

Because of the sudden mists it is foolish, whatever the weather, to venture far onto any of these moors without proper equipment. That should include:

> Maps and compasses
> A second jersey
> A woollen hat
> Waterproof kagool or smock and waterproof trousers
> Emergency rations – I favour small oranges and raisins
> A whistle – the danger signal is six blasts

The other danger to be encountered on the moors is man-made. It arises from the use of a large section of Dartmoor, and smaller areas of Bodmin, as army ranges. A red flag should be flown when these ranges are in use, but it is wise to approach them with extreme caution at all times. The Dartmoor National Park Information Centres can provide a list of the authorized dates when firing will certainly *not* be taking place.

The army are by no means the only authority to have rights on these moors, many acres of which are the preserve of the Forestry Commission. Small sections of Penwith have been bought and preserved by the National Trust, which also owns

Stone Row, Merrivale

Rough Tor on Bodmin, and certain parts of Dartmoor not protected by the National Park, which has jurisdiction over most of the moor.

This means that on Penwith and Bodmin you are nearly always walking through privately owned land, and so you should keep to the mapped footpaths as far as possible. Even on Dartmoor there is no 'common land' as such, for the grazing rights are still carefully regulated. The Country Code is just as applicable here as it is through meadow footpaths in more populated parts of the country. There may be fewer gates to be careful about, but it is just as vital not to leave any rubbish behind you, particularly in the shape of bottles, tins and plastic bags, which can cause death or serious injury to animals, as well as being intensely disrespectful to the wild beauty of the moors.

133

Dartmoor, near Two Bridges

Bibliography

Many of the books which make the best companions for anybody exploring the moors of the Southwest were written about the turn of the century, and have now fortunately been republished. Although they are obviously no longer reliable as walking guides, and although they describe a countryside that has often been sadly altered by the increase in tourism since the last war, they also lead the reader to remote places, embedded in history and prehistory, which have changed little since these writers knew them.

The books I most strongly recommend are:

W. H. Hudson, *The Land's End* (1908; reissued by Wildwood House, 1981)

Sabine Baring-Gould, *A Book of the West: Cornwall* (1899; reissued by Wildwood House, 1981)

Sabine Baring-Gould, *A Book of Dartmoor* (1900; reissued by Wildwood House, 1982)

William Crossing, *Guide to Dartmoor* (1912; reissued by David & Charles, 1976)

M. A. Courtney, *Cornish Feasts and Folklore* (1890; reissued by the Folklore Society, 1973)

Among the more recent books to which I am indebted, and which I should like to recommend to visitors to Devon and Cornwall, are those of the Sticklepath writer Douglas St Leger Gordon, most of whose books were published during the 1950s, F. E. Halliday's *A History of Cornwall* (Duckworths, second edition, 1975), Vian Smith's *Dartmoor* (Hale, 1966), Robin Davidson's *Cornwall* (Batsford, 1978), E. C. Axford's *Bodmin Moor* (David & Charles, 1975), and Gerald and Sylvia Priestland's *West of Hayle River* (Wildwood House, 1980). I have also had much pleasure from Murray's *Handbook for Devon and Cornwall* (1895; reissued by David & Charles, 1971). It makes up for any lack of literary style by its plethora of anecdote, comment and detailed information.

Index

Index

Index

Index